"Jeff Cox is a natural storyteller with a knack for weaving in the key elements. The narrative has a focus that makes the message ring loud and clear.

Ronald R. Jackson
President & CEO, Girard-Perregaux
TRADEMA of America, Inc.

"This is a very worthwhile and heart-felt book that illuminates the nuts and bolts of a subject—selling—with a refreshing humility and an eye toward what's really important in life."

Landon J. Napoleon
Author of the debut novel *ZigZag*,
which received widespread critical
acclaim and was made into a feature film.

"Being successful in business, selling, and life is all about building personal relationships with people through understanding wants, needs, and desires and fulfilling them. Rather than the focal point, 'The Big Sale' becomes a natural extension of the relationship. With incredible insight into this process, Contagious Passion clearly distinguishes itself from other 'how-to' sales books by clarifying this perspective that so many people miss."

Randy French
CEO, SurfTech

"Very few people are capable of putting into words the feelings and experiences that Jeff has with this recollection of personal memories packed with humor, insight, and knowledge."

Federico Richard
Founding Editor of *Enpunto* Magazine
Guatemala City, Guatemala

"Jeff's new book explains not only what works in luxury retail sales—but why. His unique way of teaching via stories, metaphors, and analogies is highly engaging and provides valuable insights for sales professionals who want to improve their performance."

Martin Shanker
President, Shanker Inc.

"Contagious Passion should be required reading for anyone in sales. Jeff reveals powerful selling tools in an easy-to-identify format. I read the book cover-to-cover and was left wanting more of his inspiring insights."

Carol Olsen
Partner, Hawaiian Socks

To Mary

To FRED,
My long time
friend.

Respectfully,
Jeff
July 2011

CONTAGIOUS PASSION

by Jeffrey Cox

HOW TO TAP YOUR INNER POWER AND SELL MORE

iUniverse, Inc.
New York   Bloomington

Contagious Passion
How to Tap Your Inner Power and Sell More

Copyright © 2010 Jeffrey R.Cox

iUniverse books may be ordered through booksellers or by contacting:

iUniverse
1663 Liberty Drive
Bloomington, IN 47403
www.iuniverse.com
1-800-Authors (1-800-288-4677)

ISBN: 978-1-4502-2292-1 (pbk)
ISBN: 978-1-4502-2290-7 (cloth)
ISBN: 978-1-4502-2291-4 (ebook)

Printed in the United States of America

iUniverse rev. date: 6/16/10

Chapters

Foreword

To those of you searching to improve your professional sales ability swiftly and dramatically, look no further; this book is for you. This promise, however, includes an unusual warning because should you dare to take this entire journey cover to cover, the impact on you and every personal relationship in your life will be profound.

Contagious Passion is a guidebook for selling and, more importantly, living. What you won't find here is an old-fashioned sales textbook that motivates in the moment and then quickly fades to obsolescence once you're absorbed in another busy workday. The challenge is to recognize the full scope of this journey as you begin reading the opening stories.

Jeff Cox begins with his reflective message and never lets up. His "road warrior" lessons are eloquently told and combine the often-missed collective link between sales and deep human connection. In a nuts-and-bolts world focused on the tangible, it might be easy to dismiss this text as New Age and too "touchy feely." That would be a mistake because this is a very worthwhile book.

In fact, dare yourself right now to make a commitment, a promise that what challenges us is also what makes us look within and, ultimately, is the path to becoming better people. And better people have more tools to sell effectively. This voyage of discovery begins now, so commit that you'll read the entire book front to back. And when you do so, be prepared for something wonderful as you allow yourself to move out into deeper water.

For it is there that Jeff Cox's profound and gentle message will quietly shine through and reflect back new possibilities you never knew existed.

—Landon J. Napoleon
Author of fiction and non-fiction books,
including the critically-acclaimed novel *ZigZag*,
which became a feature film

Prologue

My long journey and search for complex answers to simple questions eventually led me to the penning of this book. With my arms comfortably folded, I stood on stage awaiting a response to one of those very same questions, one I had posed so many times in the past, at just the right moment during my sales seminars, to collectively snap an audience out of complacency.

My goal: to obliterate comfort zones. And the tactical question to do just that: "How do I feel?" So innocuous and yet so powerful. Silence blanketed the gathering of professionals seated before me in the mammoth conference room. Of course, the awkward pause always evoked uncomfortable grimaces, requisite rustling, and various shifting postures. I have posed this same question to hundreds of audiences over the years of my public speaking career, and by now I'm able to fully enjoy and experience the crushing weight of stillness that makes so many people squirm. It's pain with a purpose.

I actually tap into this awkward pause to add impact to my next comment, a powerful follow-up and punch line for its predecessor. Of course, unbeknownst to me at the time was that after all the intervening years and all those seminars—during which I was casually lobbing my killer question grenade onto unsuspecting audiences—it was about to be I who would try to unravel the gnawing query. "How do I feel?" I asked for a third and final time.

Finally, a woman seated in the back row raised her hand. "We don't know how you feel, Jeff," she said, sounding as if unsure of her answer. "Are you happy, sleepy ... hung over?" With that, a relieving burst of laughter rippled through the room.

"No ..." I said, smiling and admiring her courage. "Although that's a great answer, it's not quite there." I paused to let the group settle back in. "If you will allow me to ask you one more time, but this time I will pose the question a little differently and expand on it: How does it feel to be listening to me? How do I feel to you?

"Do I feel like I am passionate about my subject to you? Does it feel like each one of you matters to me, that I care whether or not you learn something important from this seminar today? Do I feel like I am sharing this message with you for the very first time, or does it feel like I'm just going through the motions as though I've given this sales seminar a thousand times before and I'm just here to collect a paycheck?" I went on to suggest that when we choose to work in the public as salespeople, the question, "How do I feel?" might be the most important one we'll ever ask ourselves. Truly, "How do I feel?" has become my all-encompassing secret sales weapon.

It always slices right through audiences all over the world because most salespeople focus their energies elsewhere. Most people think about how they look to their customer with that long list of the intangibles: dress and appearance, confidence, knowledge, and professionalism. Few have ever considered things from the other side and how they, as the salesperson, feel to their customer. Here's the big breakthrough: as salespeople we are each activating and responsible for the feelings the customer experiences during the sales presentation. Again, that means I am (1) activating and (2) responsible for what you feel during my sales presentation. And the easiest way there? Forget trying to remember nineteen different ways to handle objections and all those closing techniques.

Keep it simple with that one little question—*how do I feel?* Over the years I have become keenly aware that it's vastly more important to the customer how a salesperson feels to them, the customer, than just about anything else. This intuitive feeling the customer gets goes beyond the standard expectations we all carry: that the salesperson be an expert in their field, that the salesperson be friendly and helpful without being pushy, that the salesperson is trustworthy, and so on. Of course, these factors need to be in place, but on a much deeper level, customers also expect to feel that they matter to the salesperson. No customer will ever say, "Do I really matter to you, Ms. Salesperson?" But believe me, they feel it. That's a core human need—we all want to matter to others on a fundamental level. In my experience the simple question of, "How do I feel?" zeroes in on the core of this issue and connects us to our customers on a deeper human level.

At least, that was the message I intended to share with my audience. On this particular day during this particular speech, however, something happened to change all that. On this day, "How do I feel?" turned itself around and unleashed its power on me. It became not so much a question about our effect on our customers and improving our level of service, but rather a question about the effect we each have on everyone with whom we come into contact every day of this life. It was such a powerful realization in that moment that I literally had to grab the lectern to steady myself and take a step back. Suddenly, the most important question in sales and customer service had morphed into the magical key that quite possibly could unlock every door to every question we might ever ask ourselves in life. How do I feel … to everyone? How do I feel as a listener when someone is speaking to me? How do I feel as a friend with whom one might share a personal feeling; a hidden fear; or bountiful joy, hope, and love? Or how about if they shared a deep feeling of personal loss, regret, and sadness? How do I feel when what you are sharing with me isn't particularly interesting to me? How do I feel to someone who can't offer me anything other than their humanity?

Suddenly, I began to tremble as my normally confident voice began to crack and strain. Standing before this distinguished audience, I felt a surge of anguish that I was somehow short-changing them; I had something real and life-changing to share, and this was likely the only moment we'd ever have together. As their speaker, I refused to take the easy way out. In a flash I decided to share this gateway to both improving sales and customer service along with all of our relationships. There was a shift in the universe that day for me. Nothing would ever be the same again, and although I didn't know it at the time, that day was also the original seed of the book you're now holding. It is a book about being better at what we do, yes, but even more important, it is a book about being a better human being.

Regardless of where today falls in your own personal journey, perhaps this moment can be the one that marks a new beginning, a simple breakthrough that changes it all. Although we may, we don't have to summit the highest mountains and find the wisest sages in stained robes to make a shift. It really can be as simple as one little question that takes the focus off ourselves. *Contagious Passion: How to Tap Your Inner Power and Sell More* is about recognizing the powerful connection between established sales concepts and your ability to apply those same skills to improve, transform, and transcend your relationships with those around you. I have been a sales professional in one form or another since the summer of 1974. I've traveled the world, had great years and tough years, and loved the journey more than anything else. My passion and purpose in this life is clearly this profession and, most importantly, the human element of connection it provides us daily.

That's a long way of saying I am not a writer by trade, so my presentation of these concepts has a single, clear purpose: to entertain you with the story while illuminating the universal message. In sharing these same stories in various forms with other salespeople over the years, I was always prodded and encouraged to gather them together between the covers of a book. These are true stories; some are composites of different events assembled together. All stem from the same point of view, a point of view where you are the starting point to your new and improved life. That place is where your inner spark ignites a blaze that catches and spreads throughout your entire life and affects all with whom you come into contact. When that happens, you'll find you spend your days in a world surrounded by wonderful people.

Wonderful people you created!

Jeff Cox
San Francisco, California
May 2009

"If you could only sense

how important you are

to the lives of those you meet;

how important you can be to the

people you may never even dream

of. There is something of yourself

that you leave at every meeting

with another person."

15

Chapter One

CONTAGIOUS PASSION

It was in Dallas, 1985, under a canopy of North Texas stars, that it finally hit me—I had become addicted to a motivational "yo-yo" diet.

I glanced about at my peers now locked away, too, in their automotive bubbles. Just moments ago they had been, as I was, fist-pumping positive and ready to conquer the world. Now their faces contorted and flashed calculated glares as the competition heated to merge onto the LBJ Highway. The two-hour revival meeting hadn't created any lasting change beyond the parking lot.

Why had this happened again? Why the temporary boost of emotion quickly followed by the predictable letdown (even moments after the big event)? Would I ever find and sustain the high level of motivation the most successful salespeople seemed to grasp?

As questions such as these have stalked me through life, I inevitably turned back to the pull of motivational books: *The Power of Positive Thinking*, by

Dr. Norman Vincent Peale; *How to Win Friends and Influence People*, by Dale Carnegie; *How I Raised Myself from Failure to Success in Selling*, by Frank Betcher. I devoured motivational seminars with famous speakers such as Zig Ziglar, like the one I'd just dropped seventy-five dollars to see.

There he was in the flesh, his dynamic performance crackling with verbal flames of fiery passion like some other-worldly preacher berating his followers on the consequences of their ways. Surely, if ever there was a fire-and-brimstone motivational speaker who could snap me out of my malaise, it was Zig Ziglar, the master of all masters.

But in the end, after Ziggy beat me down and tried to build me back up like some raw recruit, after every book was read and shelved again, every seminar attended, every conversation with a "sales expert" hashed over and over in my mind, I felt that same hollow pain and wondered again why fleeting bouts of motivation were all I could conjure.

Under the suffocating heat of that Texas night in my Jeep Cherokee, I resigned myself to this workable destiny. Stumbling through stacks of motivational books, tapes, and seminars, always pressing onward, the real key was always elusive and never permanently took up residence within. There were certainly worse fates in life.

And so, much like a quirky friend, motivation would just show up unexpectedly at my doorstep. This would be our relationship for the next nineteen years, and I was quite thankful for whatever amounts of time motivation granted me during these brief stays.

But then, during a quiet evening in 2004, my search ended. While reading a bedtime story to my granddaughter on the subject of trees, she asked me the kind of question only kids can conceive: "Do trees breathe?"

"They do," I began, "but not like we do. Trees breathe in carbon dioxide and breathe out oxygen as a by-product. Humans do just the opposite. So people and trees help each other live."

Later that evening after saying prayers and putting her to bed, I began to wonder. What did I desperately need to survive as a professional salesperson?

That's easy; motivation, of course. Tell me something I don't know, right?

CONTAGIOUS PASSION

I then thought, *Well, could this emotion be the by-product of another emotion that already exists within me?*

Rather than attempting to generate and maintain motivation, which had proven exhausting for me and, quite frankly, for everyone else I knew, I wondered if perhaps there was a source of perpetual motivation that was simply the by-product of another human emotion I already possessed.

Then the answer came to me in a single word: passion. That universal portal, that door one must discover and pass through to experience an eternal state of effortless motivation.

The one word became three: aim for passion!

As long as passion exists, it automatically converts emotion into boundless motivation. Passion and motivation are eternally linked—in seeking one you find the other, *but* your search must be ordered correctly.

- Find your passion first.
- Then you have found your source of eternal motivation.

Amazingly, passion grants perpetual motivation as a by-product to those who seek it. Rather than manufacturing motivation, let your passion be the source and generator for you like the world's most powerful energy factory. It's a package deal, and best of all, it's effortless.

I had reached a turning point in my life. Without hesitation, I chose cold turkey to leave the pack and the endless motivational marathon I had bound myself to for so many years. I would set my new life course towards a single purpose: passion. Soon passion became my lighthouse perched high upon a stony cliff to guide me through the treacherous seas of life.

This book serves as my journal, a collection of places visited, sights seen, and wonderfully colorful characters encountered. Each experience has enlightened my understanding, guiding me along my journey, and peeling off the layers, one by one, onward towards my destiny. I became determined to invest whatever precious time I possessed to seek out and engage in those things of true value.

As you will see by reading this collection of stories, I have discovered my own personal Holy Grail, my eternal source of endless passion and motivation. It had been furtively concealed from me in plain sight, surrounding my entire life. It lay in the people with whom I share my precious time on earth.

Finally, I discovered something else along the way: it is true that passion produces motivation, but passion, too, is simply a by-product of love. So to find your passion, start your journey with love. It is my sincere hope that you, too, will discover passion in life as I have, that your motivation will be generated eternally by the passion you discover. By leaving yourself, you will find yourself. Through giving, you will receive.

"When work, commitment and pleasure
all become one and you reach
that deep well where passion lives,
nothing is impossible."
Anonymous

Chapter Two

REFLECTION PROTECTION

On a brisk December evening in 1958, I witnessed my first miracle. I was eight years old, my cap and jacket were scattered under a bush and lost, and I was chilled to my core even after a demanding neighborhood game of kick-the-can. A larger dilemma loomed: I had completely lost track of time and was late for dinner. I looked into my future and cringed at the booming death knell of my mother's voice as I tried to creep unnoticed back into the house—"You're late for dinner!"

So I ran. Sprinting down the gravel road towards home, each footstep sent a loud crunch and scattered pebbles into the night. Buster, our neighbor's vigilant, one-eyed boxer, heard the familiar footfalls and began his guttural bark from behind the six-foot wooden fence separating his menacing threat from mankind.

It was an unsettling bark, however, if only to those who didn't know Buster. Beyond the specter of bodily harm conjured by the booming bark, the only possible harm Buster might administer on some poor intruder was drowning by way of full-on slobbering licks.

"It's just me, Buster!" I yelled, the same greeting shouted since I could walk and speak.

At this very moment, an arresting sight snared my gaze. I froze. My frail chest heaved billowing fog against the night air, and a little cloud formed around me as I stood transfixed. A miraculous Christmas tree (as defined by an eight-year-old) stood in the grand front window of the only two-story house in our neighborhood. It was bursting radiant light and shards of vivid color, and it was adorned in glistening multi-colored globes, garlands, and hand-strung popcorn strands. There were bubbling lights of splashy colors and gobs of silver tinsel, and the tree was crowned with a gleaming star perched atop its crest.

Then it happened. This tree began transforming itself through a rainbow of assorted colors—vivid candy apple red, fresh green grass, morning sky blue, spring daffodil yellow, and climaxing with flying saucer silver. How could an entire Christmas tree change colors? This simply boggled my eight-year-old mind. But, again, I was late for dinner and had to speed onward to face the judge and jury.

My answer to the miracle tree came a few nights later, when my mother and I walked down the street to visit Mr. and Mrs. Finchum (the owners of the house and, hence, the magical tree). As the three adults sat in the dining room discussing the events of the day, I quietly snuck, unnoticed, into the living room to give said tree a closer investigation.

Standing sentry before the large plate-glass window, the tree simply ignored my curiosity and continued changing its colors. I shot a glance toward the adults to see if they, too, were seeing this miracle, but they were unfazed. After some more detective work and poking around, I observed a small contraption on a stand placed on the floor in front of the tree.

The odd bit of hardware consisted of a large wheel with five panels of bright cellophane in red, blue, green, clear, and yellow. Tucked behind this wheel was a spotlight beaming up at the colored panels.

Although small, the little spotlight bulb was powerful enough to saturate the tree with each panel of vivid color. The mystery of the miracle had been cracked: the tree was being transformed through the power of reflection. Or, put another way—reflection dictated the color of the tree. Eureka! I had closure.

It occurred to me that this Christmas tree possessed no inherent color. Sure, it was silver when the spotlight was turned off, but it was more like a mirror than the real silver color I had in my crayon box at home. For this tree to reveal mutable colors, it borrowed them from the turning wheel. The color of the tree was dictated by the colors cast upon it. And that was about the end of giving over any further cognition to the tree.

It wasn't until many years later, at about age seventeen, that the significance of all this revealed a deeper message to me. In an effort to please everyone else in my life, I had given up my true color, the color I was meant to be, bit by bit, brush stroke by brush stroke. Eventually, I had become a walking mirror. I was colorless.

I now presented a reflection of the color I was supposed to be whenever someone came along and doused me with the tint they thought best suited me. They must know more than I, right? They were, after all, people who appeared to know better than I, people who presented a very confident opinion of who and what I was to become.

I became quite good at this reflection business. In fact, this ability served as a survival technique; it was great for getting along with others, great for never rocking the boat, great for avoiding conflicts. But it wasn't great for finding and presenting my true color. I had, without conscious thought, bargained away my true essence and become a patchwork of what others needed me to be. I had become the magic Christmas tree!

Chapter Three

FINDING TRUE COLOR

When one goes through life as only a watery reflection of what others think, there's always a gnawing sense that somewhere deep inside the soul is paying a heavy toll. And yet, one day I sensed—no matter how clever I was, no matter whom I fooled—I would ultimately become the color I was meant to be; my true color would rise up and shine forth. But from elementary school through high school the "reflection protection" mask served me well. Good with the good guys, bad with the bad guys, got along well with almost everyone.

The only area where my system lagged was in closer personal relationships. I would start off every relationship as a contrived personality. I would draw from thousands of bits of personality traits and compile the persona I believed my new girlfriend wanted. This approach worked well in the beginning of every relationship. I would just become this new person. Mr. Happy Go Lucky. Mr. Cool. The Mystery Man.

The built-in problem, however, was the energy it took me to maintain this false identity. Gradually, fatigue, frustration, and resignation would lower my guard, and the girlfriend would catch glimpses of the real Jeff, who wasn't the original boyfriend she admired. By then, it was only a matter of time before this revelation ended the relationship. The questions haunted me even at age twenty—how could a guy ever keep up this perfect front? Then again, why did a guy have to keep up this perfect front? That's when I witnessed my second miracle.

It was a postcard-standard California day: seventy-five degrees, a light breeze, the azure sky full of promise. I'd dropped in to see my friend Anne, whose house was just two blocks from mine (mine being a small, refurbished garage three blocks from the beach). While we chatted in her kitchen over a cup of organic tea, she asked me if I knew a girl named Heidi, a very cute girl who lived on the other side of the tracks from us—the side where you didn't have to live in a garage and worry about how to pay your rent each month.

"Of course I know Heidi."

"Well," Anne said, "Heidi told me that if you asked her out tonight she would go out with you."

That was all I needed to hear. I thanked Anne for the tea, hopped back into my 1963 green Volkswagen bug, and buzzed home to make the call. The good fortune—I was going out on a date with Heidi!

I remember whipping into my driveway, bolting from my car, and trotting down the driveway as I glanced over the short fence that separated my house from the neighbor's. At that moment I spotted three beautiful girls seated in beach chairs, enjoying the warm sun and friendly conversation on the backyard lawn. The bounty of life in California, it seemed, never relented. Although I had never seen the girl seated in the middle of the three, something struck a chord in me, and in that moment—even with the well-heeled Heidi on slate—I knew that I wanted to spend the rest of my life with this mystery girl!

So I went against all my previous history and hopped the short fence, sauntered across the grass right up to the girls, and introduced myself. During that brief stroll I had already made a decision I would never regret: I decided to just be Jeff. Amazingly, three hours later we were still sitting on the lawn on that glorious sun-splashed day. Heidi wasn't even a vague memory at that point; she had left my consciousness completely. And then I did it—I asked this new girl to marry me. And much to my delight, the mystery girl, Mary Catherine Wheeler, said, "Yes."

Mary informed me that her father was in fact "at sea" on the day we met—he was a merchant sailor by trade—so it would be just over a year before we were finally able to tie the knot. The ceremony was on June 24, 1973, at precisely 3 p.m. in the Santa Maria Chapel, a quaint structure perched high upon a bluff overlooking the Pacific Ocean. Both families, including my soon-to-be father-in-law, were in attendance.

After the simple ceremony and festivities wound down, we settled into a small cottage that sat on the same piece of property where we'd met the year prior. It was there we began the task of building a new life together, including the planting of our first of countless vegetable gardens. We grew carrots, squash, zucchini, corn, and tomatoes. It wasn't long before our neighbors began avoiding the newlyweds for fear of being handed more sacks teeming with vegetables.

This was an extraordinary time in our lives. Mary and I were in our early twenties and madly in love, and our lifetimes stretched out before us like a lazy cat on a sun-drenched windowsill. We looked forward with great joy to building our family and spending our entire lives together.

Fast forward: Mary and I have now been married for thirty-six years and have adult children of our own. Over the years our children have asked me for advice about their relationships. Generally, these inquiries surfaced as they were getting their hearts trampled and because their mother and I get along so effortlessly. They felt we held some sort of special secret key to this complicated relationship deal.

My answer would always start with the same question: "Are you being your true color, presenting your true self?" Our children understood this question, as we had stressed the importance of being you no matter the circumstances. I would share with them that whenever you mix two people together, as in a relationship, it's similar to mixing two colors of paint. Certain combinations just don't work. I shared with them that on the day their mother and I met I risked being my true color, which I have always pictured as bright blue. Mary, their mother, I envision as vivid yellow.

So the key to the success of our coupledom is that our two primary colors, because both parties entered into the relationship as their true selves, form a glorious green. This synergistic shade is more extraordinary than either of the individual primary colors could ever be. My advice: never attempt to adjust either your color or theirs. Finally, I would remind my kids that some color combinations never produce a beautiful, harmonious tint no matter how long you stir and shake the can.

My fatherly advice always ended with a solemn promise. If they always present to the world their true self and true color, even if doing so may cause them occasional pain, when they finally connect with the right person, their love will be real. And the new color that they and their loved one create together will last a lifetime. As an extra bonus, they will love the ease of being themselves whenever they are together.

Be courageous and risk being you. Enter into every relationship in your life not with bells and whistles to impress but a real color shining outward. The real you is what's most impressive. If things work out from that place, that will be wonderful. If not, then you never could have adjusted yourself or the other to make it last. You'll be glad; it's exhausting to maintain a false persona. That Christmas tree on a cool evening in 1958 still reminds me how easy it is to flash unreal images.

It takes courage to be your true self, your true color, and the person you are destined to be. But this will be the beginning to your new life, your true life, the life that plugs perfectly into the grand scheme of things. This new life started for me on a sunny California day in a small backyard.

How about yours?

Chapter Four

FATHER

I watched my father die, and I've never felt so powerless. What began as a diagnosis of mesothelioma in the fall of 1997 in California ended a year later with a eulogy in a church perched on an Oregon river bank.

Mesothelioma is a difficult word to spell and pronounce, and it is even tougher to comprehend when it reverberates through the hospital room as the diagnosis delivered to one's father. The doctor explained the term as a form of cancer almost always caused by asbestos exposure. My father could only shake his head—at seventeen years old he was in the navy during World War II. The ship hulls emitted an inescapable fog of toxic asbestos fibers. Decades later, there could be no amount of money, tears, prayers, or anguish that would reverse the damage; asbestos would collect in full. And thus began my father's inexorable freefall into death's gaping maw. All any of us could do was watch.

Throughout those final days and weeks, his warm, roguish eyes lost their brash, blue spirit and faded into a fatigued and distant grey. I watched his hands—once calloused, rough, and robust, each with a powerful grip—

gradually turn soft and frail. His sturdy wrists, too, were gaunt, skeletal reminders of his once-formidable presence. Looking outward from the farthest corner of the family room, he had taken to resting, still and tranquil, cocooned in his well-stuffed, favorite chair. As I watched him, there was a palpable and steady draining away of all he had been.

Since childhood, I've seen my father as an impressive character ripped from the pages of Patrick O'Brian's *Master and Commander*—larger than life, always bursting with verve, zest, and zeal. Then, as that heroic vitality and vigor slowly seeped out, I saw only this lingering shell shrinking ever smaller until his splendid sparkle had simply vanished.

Always vibrant in his golden South Pacific tan, his massive shoulders, authoritative arms, and salty sailor's legs wore scores of tattoos that, when decoded correctly, told dazzling tales of heavy seas and barroom brawls from Frisco to Hong Kong, Singapore, and back. On certain nights, when the stars aligned just right and with the Hennessey poured to the proper level, my father would discreetly divulge one or two of these trans-Pacific tales to a privileged few.

In rage his voice would send shivers down to any soul in earshot, while in moments of counsel, he was the texture and tone of a holy man. His mind crisp and alert up until those final weeks, he carved out seventy-four years and was a Pearl Harbor and battleship survivor. He lived a man's life of strong feats and deeds with many more tales to spin if only allowed a bit more time. But instead, my father was about to die.

All through those last days, nestled in that tattered, olive green chair, my father welcomed each visitor with his warm smile. These visitors began to notice a startling change in the rogue adventurer. Without hesitation, he was candidly petitioning the people he loved for their forgiveness, making amends for mistakes he may have made along the way. Rather than making this appeal in a weepy or whimpering way, my father simply gazed into each person's eyes, asked for amnesty, and granted them pardon in return. It was all so very simple; he had cleaned his slate.

By banishing those barriers, he had magically and unconditionally transformed both his head and his heart. All those faces he had known and cared for throughout his life had finally been allowed inside his private fortress of confident swagger. The unpretentious act of engaging others in expressions of appreciation and recognition allowed him to communicate, not as a courageous mentor-protector, but simply as a man speaking from the heart, unguarded, without reserve or restraint.

He spoke from a place of appreciation—an appreciation for each person living and each moment passing—an appreciation for every precious breath and every heartbeat. Choosing to be fully alive and in the moment, without precondition and with no status or strata considered, he had finally recognized the true nature of his happiness. He had discovered appreciation.

For Dad, all persons traveling through his sphere had become precious. And, as he finally embraced and accepted the brief, fleeting beauty and sadness of life, he knew, too, that every person truly mattered. Judgments, comparisons, internal chatter, and resentments ... all were notions that no longer mattered. In the narrowing twilight space of his life, there was no longer a spare moment to be wasted on trivial themes. And, he realized, there never had been.

Finally, the cold, gray day came—an Oregon morning. Birds ruffled against each other for warmth as a muddle of soft rain and sleet pelted the parlor window of a white, clapboard cottage on Independence Avenue in the small town of Monmouth, Oregon. As I sat and held his hand, I knew our time together had come to an end; my father was gone. During those last days, I had seen him evolve even further from the man he had been all his life. He had found the voice of his heart. And although he never said it, I believe he finally became the man that he wished he'd always been.

His departure raised many questions. Why do we wait so long to do what's real and important? Why do we wait so long to change? Why do we wait right until the end to improve our conditions, our relationships, and, ultimately, ourselves? What day on the calendar are we waiting for so that we might begin to make our lives what we believe they can be?

Searching the dial of my wristwatch and the face of the wall clock, I find no specific hour designated as the hour for change. That must mean, then, that we can choose to change at any hour in the day, on any day in our lives. If change is afoot, then I ask myself, "Who do I wish to become?" A man named Mahatma Gandhi advocated that we "become the change [we] seek." Were we to truly benefit from this sage advice, we might continually encourage each other to always seize the moment, for we never know when that cold, gray shadow of our final chapter will appear. That's when my father found his change—right at the end of the journey. What if we, instead, resolve to be the warm sun ... today ... right now?

What is real and important to you?

If your life were to end tonight at midnight, if today was in fact *that day,* how would you spend your last day on earth? What words would you choose to say to your loved ones, friends, strangers, and even yourself? How would you treat the people who crossed your path on *that day?*

Imagine on *that day* you stepped from your house to collect the mail and encountered the postal employee. What might you say to her on *that day?* How might you treat her knowing it would be the last time you'd ever see her?

Or, in your car and on your way, how would the other drivers on the road affect you on *that day?* Would you get agitated or frustrated if a driver forgot to use a turn signal, drove too slow or too fast, or pulled out of a side street and cut you off? Or might these all suddenly seem wholly trivial?

Imagine on *that day* arriving at the gas station to find every pump occupied. Would you curse, fret, and tap your foot if they decided to take a little more time to wash the windshield or get the kids secured with the endless straps in the safety seats?

Today is *that day!* Since it is always today, it will be on a "today" that you will die. Consider this fact: from the dying person's perspective, not once in human history has anyone ever died yesterday or tomorrow. Today is our day for living, loving, learning, listening, and changing, and today is also our day for dying. Everything in life ultimately occurs on a "today." What can you do *today* to become the person you want to be?

Is there one person you might call now to ask for amnesty? Someone you know you've wanted to forgive for a past misdeed? What about yourself— have you forgiven yourself today for being imperfect? When we do this important business of cleaning our own spiritual slate, new possibilities open up before us. And just like my father learned, it's all so very simple.

Chapter Five

THE ROOKIE

"They're all pretty nice except one guy named Mike Young. He's pretty much a jerk."

It was late one weeknight, August 1973, and my wife Mary and I were wrapping up our nightly phone call. Having accepted a new job two hours from home, I was ensconced in a marginal hotel for the duration of my three-month, probationary training period. If all went well, I would be promoted and moved to a permanent store, at which time my wife would join me. If all did not go well, I would be, well, unemployed.

The nightly call home, at exactly 10:00 p.m. with a firm time limit of three minutes per call (I had reams of training material to get through every night), was less about relaying daily minutiae and more about just hearing her voice. I savored this daily emotional touchstone.

"What do you mean, 'a jerk?'" she asked.

"Well, he's one of those guys who just makes fun of everybody on the sales floor, especially the new guy."

"Well, you can handle him," she said. "You just have to put up with him until you're transferred." As usual, she was right. She was encouraging me short-term and affirming me long-term—I'd have to still be around in three months to be transferred at all.

Changing the subject, she inquired, "So what are you doing tomorrow?"

"Tomorrow I'm going to the Lodi store for two days to cover for the manager who's on vacation."

"That sounds good."

"It should give me a chance to feel what it'll be like when I get my own store."

"Seems like a good sign. They must think a lot of you to let you take over while the manager is gone."

"I think so."

The following morning, the regional manager for my new firm climbed into his silver Mercedes coupe for the two-hour drive from San Francisco to our state's capital, Sacramento. Unbeknownst to me, his mission on that particular day: make a store visit, perform a store audit, and fire the new salesman—me. Simultaneously, I was reporting to the Sacramento store at 8:30 a.m. sharp, where I was completing my training and grabbing directions to the Lodi store for my interim post.

This was a big day for me; I was convinced everyone in the store could see I was taking this opportunity as my stamp of approval. The kid was on his way to management! After the supervisor gave me directions, I went into the back office to retrieve my sports coat. My sales training nemesis stood in the office doorway, blocking my entrance—Mike Young.

"So you're going to Lodi today?" His smile made me cringe.

"Yes, I am."

"Well, good luck!"

"Thanks," I replied, somewhat guardedly.

"And by the way," he said, his toothy grin growing even wider, "if I never see you again, I hope everything works out."

Suddenly I felt a chill run through me because either Mike Young was just holding character, or he knew something I didn't. And I was leaning toward the latter.

"What do you mean by that?"

"Well," he smirked, "whenever they send someone out to cover a store, it usually means they're history. Especially guys like you."

"Guys like me?"

"You know … guys who can't sell."

The cold sweat turned into a hot flash surging through my body. "What are you talking about? I can sell."

"No, you can't. When's the last time you even made a sale?"

"I don't know." I hesitated as I searched my memory. "Last week? Yes, I made one last week. A white gold wedding band for sixty-eight cash."

"A whole sixty-eight dollars? Let me alert corporate accounting so they're not bowled over by the revenue surge. Like I said, Jeff."

Mike was right. Although I had been trying very hard, I hadn't had much success.

"Listen, Jeff," he said. "You're a nice guy and there are probably lots of jobs you can do in your life, but selling just isn't one of them."

The feeling of devastation hit me square in the gut and pulsed outward from there. Somehow, in the span of minutes, I'd gone from the rising star to a hapless rookie with no shot at making it.

"So what do you suggest I do now?" I asked. Yes, I was fully aware that although Mike Young was a world-class jerk, he was also the best salesperson in the store. It was a hard truth to swallow.

"Jeff, I could see your problem the first day you arrived," he said. His evil countenance softened slightly to that of an older brother, which meant he acted more caring while retaining the subtle condescending air. "Let me share something with you that someone told me a long time ago that really helped me." He stepped closer and handed me my sport coat.

I took the jacket. While we were never going to invite each other over for a barbecue, this was a side of Mike I had never witnessed before. So I said, "Yeah, let me hear it."

"Jeff, you need to start selling jewelry part-time. And you need to sell yourself the other part."

That was the boy-genius advice? "Sell jewelry part-time, sell myself the other part? I have no idea what that means."

"Well, kid, that should give you something to think about on the drive down to Lodi." And with that, Mike Young laughed, patted me on the back, and walked away with his smug smile intact.

Of course, for the next hour and a half, as I made the drive from Sacramento to Lodi, I was haunted by Mike's advice. I began to see its truth and that, unfortunately, Mike Young was right again. I really had been trying hard to sell jewelry. After all, wasn't that my job? But, selling jewelry part-time? And selling myself the other part?

The more I pondered this apparent paradox, the more I realized that I had only been focused on jewelry—the product, not the people. I was not investing time or energy in making a connection with my customers on a personal level. I was like a selling machine spewing a precise presentation of facts, figures, and information. In that moment, I met a harsh reality: if I were a customer shopping for a piece of jewelry, or any product for that matter, the last salesperson I would buy from would be someone who took no personal interest—*zero*—in the customer. Namely, me.

I thought back to things purchased, from a lawnmower to a new suit, and how much better it felt when the salesperson took an interest in my needs and made time to connect with me on a personal level. Indeed, that single quality was one of the main reasons I bought something from one salesperson over another. Personal connection. I've even paid a little more for a product just because of the salesman.

As I sat in the slow lane on Interstate 5, I vowed to myself that from the moment I entered the Lodi store, and for the rest of my selling career, I would sell myself every time I sold anything, and that a personal connection would be the most important part of every sale I ever made. Even if a customer decided not to buy my product for whatever reason, I would make sure that they bought *me*.

The wheels of my VW hit the parking lot, and minutes later I entered the Lodi store. I noticed a customer standing by the diamond counter, waiting for assistance. I walked up to him and introduced myself. From that moment on, I remembered my vow to make the human connection the single most important element of the interaction. "Selling" was not even on my radar because, indeed, the human connection is the sale. Not just because it would enhance my sales performance, which it did, but also because it enhances my customer's experience. Thanks to Mike Young, things turned for me that day. I was not summarily dismissed; I fulfilled the two-day interim position with new flair and success.

So, what had changed about my ability to sell, my confidence level, and my attitude? Everything changed the moment I began to view the sale from this totally new vantage point: my sales presentation was not about convincing the customer to make a purchase so that I might close the sale, hit my sales goals, and ultimately keep my job.

Result vs. reason

My needs were no longer the focus of attention, and it was this shift that sparked a new way of viewing the sales process. Suddenly, making the sale was a natural result of treating my client correctly, not the *reason* to do so!

Rather than attempting to create a favorable *action from* clients through the presentation of features and benefits, I aimed for a more deep-rooted *reaction within* clients by tapping into their emotions. Though I do not possess the power to control my client's actions (decision making), I can have a role in creating an emotional reaction in people.

Selling myself was the most effective pathway to doing so. From *selling ourselves,* we can all easily make the leap to the real goal: *selling them.*

It's all about them.

In life and in selling, it is all about them: your clients, your life partner, your kids, your friends, and everyone else. Most of us get this switched around, instead focusing on the product. That approach never works as well.

What a relief it was to discover that "selling myself" took the mind off the product and shifted it to emphasizing a real human connection; that's a much easier primary goal. With that in mind, what is the best way to quick and deep human connections with strangers?

We all know that the choice to join the selling profession will place us each before a constant stream of strangers, most of whom are naturally defensive and suspicious. Don't we all react the same way whenever a slick salesperson attempts to convince us this new Product X is the greatest thing money can buy? Conversely, if you choose connection over product, you'll want to learn to locate a conversation's ground zero.

Discovering ground zero

What if you could establish a repeatable mental platform guaranteed to 1) create a predictable environment within your client's mind, 2) whisk you past natural, human resistance, and 3) establish immediate trust? Might that be a better foundation for each sales presentation?

We've all experienced fleeting moments of *ground zero*, where client and salesperson just "click" during certain sales presentations. Those are the times when the job is more than selling and, better yet, feels fantastic to both parties! Consider the possibility that every conversation might contain a *conversational ground zero*. Imagine the possibilities.

Getting to ground zero is not as difficult as you might think. For starters, following are three things to try the next time you meet with a client.

Imagination

Since you will most likely become friends with your client *after* he or she makes a purchase from you, why wait? Simply place this friendship at the front of the sale! Hint: the customer is going to like you.

Don't you generally make friends with all of the customers who have made purchases from you? Whenever they return for the second, third, or sixth time to your establishment, doesn't your entire relationship with them transform into one of friendship? Of course it does!

Just pretend you and the client are friends at the beginning of your presentation, which is not that hard to imagine, right? Now imagine that the two of you have carved out some time in your busy schedules to shop together for the product he or she is considering. From this point of view, your entire presentation—and your customer's experience of the selling process—is dramatically altered into a new environment you created and control!

As a friend, it is important to *you* that she (your customer) fully understands just how and why this particular product fits her needs. A friend would make certain by asking probing questions to assure she fully understands the value and benefits the product has to offer. It's really that simple.

Honesty

Operating from a platform of friendship, honesty becomes paramount. When you're on the other side of the sale—as salesperson and also friend— you are responsible for the suggestions, comparisons, and conclusions necessary for making the best buying decision. There is only one way in life we can truly move forward with certainty that our words and actions don't come back to haunt us in any way: honesty.

Risk

Your level of risk increases when your customer is your friend because you are more demanding of the facts, reasons, and convictions for making the purchase. You are invested in the final decision, and in order to justify the purchase, you must be completely and utterly convinced that this product is right for your friend.

As a friend, *you* need absolute assurance that this product fits her needs and desires; if the product does not, you are willing to walk away from the sale. Salespeople resist losing a sale; friends don't. Your customer will feel and appreciate this genuine honesty.

So by way of imagination, honesty, and risk, we establish an enhanced and secure footing. This is a repeatable mental platform to conduct your sales presentations. From there, it's much easier to discover a position of ground zero with every customer we encounter.

Eventually, I was off probation and officially posted at a new store. Then, at the close of the following year, I actually received the "Rookie Salesman of the Year" award. From there, I earned a spot in the prestigious "President's Club" for the next seven consecutive years—not bad for someone who was hours away from being canned for not being able to sell. And it all started with Mike Young, who taught me that simple and critical truth—I learned to sell my product part-time, and the rest of the time I sold *me.*

Chapter Six

MR. PERSUADER

At about the time the pistol slammed into the back of my head during a midday jewelry store heist the summer of 1976, I decided to make a career change. Yes, I was thinking, I would seek employment outside the jewelry industry.

"On the floor! Heads down! Do what I tell you!" The assailant snarled his demands through a filthy blue scarf he pressed against his face with one hand as he waved the cold-blue steel pistol towards me with his other. I found my spot on the cool, aqua tile floor alongside my fellow coworkers.

"These all the diamonds you have?"

After spending the past eight years of my life selling jewelry, I thought, *Maybe I could go back into the landscaping business. I always preferred plants to diamonds, anyway.* These career musings came with my face pressed to the cold tile.

"Where's the safe? Somebody show me the (expletive) safe now, or I'll kill everybody!" Seconds later, an employee directed him to the safe, which, fortunately although strictly against store policy, was wide open. He proceeded to empty the safe.

"I'm outta here," he said, lowering his voice for dramatic effect. "Any of you looks up, I'll kill you."

Of course, with that we all looked up only to see his receding form running down the street at a fast clip, clutching our store's diamond collection in a brown paper sack. A sack, in fact, that I recognized as one that had previously contained a tuna fish sandwich, a bag of potato chips, and M&M's, lovingly packed for me earlier that morning by my wife Mary. Good riddance, Mr. Armed Assailant. And good riddance, jewelry industry.

Within weeks of the incident, I quit my job, packed up my family, and headed north out of California to the serene, green Willamette Valley in Oregon. There we found soft, rolling fields of long grasses, family-owned farms replete with classic barns, and a booming building industry. With five brothers-in-law (another story for another book) in the construction trade, I had a new job awaiting me far from the cloying complications of city life and near-death career experiences.

After eight years in the world of rare gems and affluent clients, where fine wool suits and silk Hermes ties were my requisite daily uniform, life in the construction trade appealed to me immediately. It was liberating to walk onto the job site each day in a worn cotton T-shirt, shorts, and ball cap. The physical labor rejuvenated my soul and infused my spirit with new energy. Soon our little family settled into our new Oregonian lifestyle of hard-working days, large family weekend gatherings, and nights of deep, refreshing sleep. And best of all, odds were good that no brazen holdups ("Give me your tools!") would interrupt my new daily routine.

New to the construction trade and possessing few tools of my own, I showed up for work my first morning with only a hammer, a JC Penney special that I'd only used once—to drive a single nail into a wall to hang a framed picture in our living room. Nevertheless, department-store hammer and I arrived at precisely 6 a.m., ready to take on the day's challenge.

Leaning against a stack of lumber while casually removing a splinter from his leathery hand, Joseph Wheeler, my wife's third-oldest brother, stood positioned at the entrance of the site to greet me. JoJo, as he has been known since his youth, was a force of nature. Tall and thin, sporting limbs like bound steel strands, and complete with infectious energy and a captivating smile, JoJo had long been my favorite brother-in-law.

"So the California surfer dude showed up after all!" JoJo wasted no time in beginning the abuse, which was a construction industry version of a welcoming hug.

"Yep, ready to go." I raised my "hammer" like a warrior on the battlefield hoisting a broadsword.

"Whatcha gonna do with that thing, little brother? Hang a picture?" JoJo's laugh made me smile. I could feel my face go flush and, as usual, turn bright red.

"Yeah, I figure after you build the house, I'll go inside and hang the first picture!"

"Sounds like a good plan to me, brother." Then, more serious, JoJo's eyebrows furrowed and he said, "You know, little brother, a guy can build a house with nothing but a hammer. Probably even a toy one like that."

"Really." I couldn't tell if he was serious or just lining up the new guy for the next punch line.

"Oh yes, you can," he continued. "Dig the footer trench with the claw, then turn the hammer around and pound the nails to form it up—frame the whole house. Instead of a saw you just beat on each board with your hammer 'til it breaks to the right length." Then he let loose with the first of many world-class JoJo cackles, a warm laugh that always makes everyone around him smile, too.

Within months, I had slipped into the construction trade rhythm and routine. As my skill level increased, my waistline (much to my wife's delight) decreased. Also by this time, I owned a complete set of industry-grade tools. No more borrowing tools from one of my mates. Hammer, square, tape measure, and power saw I used all day, every day. I also had drills, sanders, and chisels. And then there was Mr. Persuader. Seldom used, Mr. Persuader had a long, yellow handle and heavy, ten-pound steel head. Mr. Persuader was a sledgehammer that generally spent the days in repose behind the front seat of my truck.

It was only on special occasions that we invited Mr. Persuader onto the site to perform duties befitting his nature. A wall was a little off plumb before we began to hang the sheetrock? I'd just go to my truck, flip the seat forward, and ask Mr. Persuader if he might assist in bringing things back to center with a gentle love tap.

So this was my tool collection. The key was that whether needed that day or not, I had them all in my toolbox. A situation would never arise in which I could not perform a task for lack of the proper tool. As each challenge presented itself during my day, I was able to reach for the proper tool to complete the task with ease. Even if I seldom had need for a particular tool, I made sure that it was in my arsenal so I would not be caught off guard.

However, as I soon discovered, people can never fully protect themselves from being caught off guard in life; life just doesn't work out that neatly. There are those inevitable moments when a simple phrase or statement uttered opens one door while simultaneously slamming another. Such statements alter the direction of our life course—a cosmic nudge that sends us off towards a completely different point on the horizon.

My "life-altering" comment came in the form of a casual declaration in our kitchen by my wife Mary while she readied sack lunches for our two boys. Over the sound of the school bus rattling up the street—a clatter that always sent birds scattering to higher perches and our cat Max to deep beneath the sofa—she said, "Honey, we're going to have a baby!"

We embraced in the center of the kitchen as the old bus clamored to a stop and blared its horn to gather up the neighborhood kids. The first thought that raced through my head as I held Mary tightly in my arms: *The lighting in our kitchen is definitely glowing a little brighter with this news.*

The sunny news of the impending arrival of a new baby also brilliantly lit the reality of the financial cloud looming directly over our house at the far end of Oakdale Drive. Over the previous months, the financial pressure mounted with the arrival of each bill. While the construction trade had slimmed my waistline, it seemed to have had the same affect on our bank account. Spiritual benefits aside, I simply was not able to support my young family on an apprentice carpenter's wages.

So, as refreshing and cleansing as my eighteen-month stint in the construction trade was, I was soon back in a wool suit, crisp white shirt, and tie, selling jewelry in an industry where I commanded much better pay as a result of my extensive experience. Within a few short years, after initially being hired as a store manager, I was promoted to regional manager at a high-end jewelry establishment called Black Starr & Frost, headquartered in Alexandria, Virginia.

It was during the fall of 1983, with Ronald Reagan in the White House, that we packed up once again, pulled our children out of school, sold our two-bedroom house in Oregon, and boarded a plane headed for our nation's capital.

Much to our delight, we found Washington DC to be a vibrant city, especially for a young family eager to learn from all the historic buildings, monuments, and museums. We spent most weekends trekking around town and to nearby sites, including George Washington's stately Mt. Vernon mansion and Civil War battlegrounds such as grassy Manassas. We peered into the balcony at Ford's Theater where President Lincoln was shot and imagined John Wilkes Booth leaping to the stage after committing his horrific act.

As for my new job, it was simply fantastic. Headquartered in historic Alexandra, Virginia, it was exciting just going to work! Before long, Mary and I were referring to the entire experience of moving our family across the country as a brilliant *working vacation*.

In my new role, I oversaw stores in seven western states and had long lists of responsibilities. The most rewarding, however, was basic sales training for some forty sales associates throughout my region. For nearly eight years, I crisscrossed the country, meeting with salespeople and evaluating their performance. Most of the time, this required listening to particular selling challenges indigenous to particular regions and then providing solutions.

About two years into my new position, I had a profound realization while driving to the airport. Rather than seeing myself as a regional manager traveling from state to state and store to store, I imagined my entire region as one large store. Instead of searching for individual solutions for each sales associate's challenges, I could simply cross-pollinate the successful selling solutions I had picked up from one store and transfer them to another store. This also proved a highly effective method for other in-store challenges, whether they were display, improved customer service, or the resolution of employee conflicts.

The overall result was an exponential improvement in employee morale, productivity, and, most importantly, selling effectiveness. For example, it was not uncommon for a sales associate in Dallas, Texas, to run into the same objection from a client that a sales associate in San Francisco had already confronted, analyzed, and resolved successfully. Suddenly, the answers to most sales challenges leapt out at me. Prior to this discovery, I had been swept up in the specific facts of the associates' stories and was missing traits common to all sales challenges. I began to zero in on common traits the salespeople were experiencing far more than facts about their individual situations. These traits were those common elements all salespeople face regardless of demographics.

Generally, trait challenges were concealed within the "facts stories" of each unique sales situation. The facts stories were usually highly charged with emotion (this was my key to recognizing them). However, trait challenges were more like patterns sans emotional attachments. A classic example was when a salesperson said, "All of my customers tell me that this watch brand is just too expensive no matter what I say; that's why I can't sell it."

First, I stripped away the emotional elements in the phrases: "all of my customers" and "just too expensive." These are words and comments charged with emotion. Second, I identified the trait in this comment, which is nothing more than price push back—i.e., price resistance, a trait common in most selling situations in most industries. Third, I suggested the use of a classic selling technique I refer to as the "that-and-this" solution, a time-based technique using a past/present structure: "That is how I used to feel; this is how I feel now." Following is how it might flow in a selling situation.

> Customer: "This watch brand is overpriced; it's just too expensive!"
>
> Salesperson: "It's interesting you say that because when this watch brand was first introduced to our store, all of us here felt very much the same way. However, after learning the components inside these watches are handmade, we now feel it is actually under-priced for what you get. Let me show you why …"

Note that the word "however" represents a new way of viewing the same thing. In this case, the trait challenge was price resistance; the solution was first agreement followed by new information. This way, the client felt validated in his belief that the watch, indeed, was too expensive. Even professional watch sales associates felt the same way! That is, until the sales associates learned more information about the product. New information changed the way the salesperson viewed the product and its asking price. Now the customer, too, learned these additional facts about the watch, and this discovery allowed him to alter his initial position of price resistance without internal conflict. Now he could view the watch under a new light just as the salespeople had and make a new decision based on these new facts.

In my experience conducting training, once the sales associates began to separate the facts of their challenges (facts charged with emotion) from the traits (unemotional basics), they could begin the process of analyzing and improving their selling methods free of any emotional interference. They began to identify basic traits.

However, as time went on, I discovered that in spite of their success, some sales associates simply would not embrace a solution to their sales challenges if it did not fit their perceived "selling style." That is to say, associates would simply resist proven solutions to their selling challenges, saying things like, "That's not my style; I could never just ask for the sale," "I'm not the pushy type; I couldn't ask a client what's stopping him or her from buying today," or even, "I just couldn't tell a client what to buy!"

This trait is fear based and reveals an avoidance of asking the client any direct or probing questions about their objections or buying decision. Why? It is fear that the *question* will scare away the client, i.e., a reluctance to drag Mr. Persuader onto the job site. Paradoxically, by not asking the question and therefore never discovering the core reasons to the client's true objections, they lose the sale anyway. These salespeople display a low tolerance for risk, and no matter how earnest their efforts, they never seem to break into the top level of sales producers.

I was becoming aware that certain salespeople limited their success in sales by viewing themselves, and their selling style, in a certain fixed way. What became most alarming to me was their inflexibility and resistance to improved selling methods and techniques. They had become bound, imprisoned even, to a specific style of selling, a sort of "one-style-sells-all" approach.

"I'm a soft-style salesperson," they would tell me. "I would rather lose a sale than be perceived as too pushy." These were adults who chose to be in our selling profession; comments like these baffled me. Late one night while flying home from yet another airport, my mind kept slamming into the same nagging question: "Why in the world would salespeople refuse to compile and collect all the selling tools available to them to be more successful?"

That's when JoJo and Mr. Persuader popped into my mind. I smiled as I recalled my time in carpentry and how important it was to assemble and own a complete toolbox. Imagine a carpenter who needed to cut a piece of lumber but said, "I'm just not a power-saw type of carpenter; I prefer a hand-saw style." He'd never finish any project! Or what if I had needed to move a wall base and someone suggested I go get Mr. Persuader out of my pickup, and I had responded, "That's not my style. I'm not a pushy carpenter! I would never use a sledgehammer on someone's home!" This type of thinking would have been viewed as absurd and gotten me laughed off the job site.

In the construction trade, I learned to *choose* the proper tool for the proper task. All tools were considered *neutral*; all tools were *equal*. Hammers, saws, measuring tapes, drills, and sledgehammer—all had equal worth because each performed a specific task, and the right tool in the hands of an expert always worked.

Therein lies the solution for selling. The tools change to adjust to certain challenges and conditions, but the carpenter remains the same. Are you normally a "soft" salesperson—very personable, more like a friend to your client? Perfect! But every once in a while, when that indecisive client comes around, do you possess the ability, the tools, to apply the command-close technique? This is a time-tested sales technique of simply telling the client to buy it. It is a technique that has worked millions of times with millions of salespeople all around the globe!

"But," you say, "I'm not a pushy salesperson."

"Well," I say, "I'm not a pushy carpenter either, but when a wall needs to be tapped an inch or two over, I don't pull out a feather duster; I go to the truck and look behind the seat for Mr. Persuader."

Think of it this way: the tools we select for each challenge do not define us. As a salesperson, you're going to come across a few clients out of every hundred who require a nudge. The guy standing in front of you at 4:45 p.m. on Christmas Eve, saying, "I just can't decide, let me think about it," needs only one thing to tip the scale: a gentle "tap" from Mr. Persuader. Don't you think this would be the time for you to use a command close? It is the time to look your client in the eye and say, *"Buy it—she'll love it!"*

Do I sell like this all the time? Of course not! I didn't go to the truck every day to get that sledgehammer, either. But, whatever the situation during the sales process, whatever my client's motivation, wherever the sale leads me, I always show up with a complete toolbox of sales techniques. You must as well.

We must possess every sales technique we can learn—hard, soft, long-winded, short, brief, firm, and friendly. All these are just different, necessary tools for different jobs. Our responsibility is to identify the client's needs and desires and then help with the proper solution. Some days it will require a low-key tap; other days will need a bigger nudge from the business end of the yellow handle.

In the normal course of illuminating the benefits of products and services, we all come up against questions, doubts, and resistance as clients make buying decisions. These are normal events; they are to be expected and not feared. Don't we all experience the same natural resistance to making a decision? I know I do. However, when I'm on the other side as a customer working with a highly skilled (not high-pressured) salesperson, I am able to navigate through the process towards the proper decision. That's because highly skilled sale professionals possess all the right tools, talents, and techniques to guide me along the path.

They have forecasted my fears, doubts, objections, and natural hesitations, and they have provided me with solutions that will prove beneficial to my final decision. They have also taken responsibility for my side—the customer's side—of the sale. Their sales presentations were well-crafted and well-presented with confidence. In fact, viewed from the customer's side, they have made it easy for me to arrive at my decision, whether it's to purchase or not.

In contrast, the experience with the high-pressure salesperson is just the opposite. One is left with the feeling that this salesperson doesn't care who is standing in front of him. There is no sense that he has invested time in viewing the sale from the customer's side. He just pounds away! Slamming up against his customer's resistance, he reminds me of what my brother-in-law JoJo said my first day on the job. These salespeople attempt to build a house with just a hammer because that's the only selling skill they possess. Having someone use the claw of a hammer to excavate my objections is not a pleasant experience for either party.

Then this salesperson flips the hammer around to pound selling points into my head. And, finally, should I not see things his way, he will commence to beat on me with the same hammer for an hour until I am broken into the proper length. Whenever I come across a salesperson employing this style of selling on me, I'm compelled to award them with a world-class JoJo cackle.

I'm also reminded to always be flexible in my own approach and use every tool in my toolbox, however infrequent, and to only pull out the yellow-handled beauty on those rare occasions when only the right tool will do—Mr. Persuader.

<blockquote>
"We make a living by what we get, we make a life by what we give."
Sir Winston Churchill
</blockquote>

Chapter Seven

PUT A SHINE ON THE DAY

Much like the guttural blasts of foghorns beckoning from nearby San Francisco Bay, the rich, unmistakable voice always preceded the captain of the St. Francis Hotel shoeshine stand. From within his post at the gentleman's salon near the far end of the grand hallway, Otis had been snapping towels on glossed leather for fifty years. A tall man—closing in on ninety, fit and strong with massive hands—his baritone voice resonated through the hotel lobby early each day and boomed a hearty good morning to passersby.

On one special morning, that same lobby was buzzing with harried hotel staff as they positioned a lectern against the far lobby wall and adjusted enormous floral displays. Noting the gathering crowds and commotion from the jewelry store I managed adjacent to the lobby, I asked my assistant, Joseph, to find out what event was on the morning docket. We were used to dignitaries and celebrities and other well-heeled clientele breezing through our midst, but it was always nice to know exactly what to expect.

After a bit, Joseph reemerged from the chaos sporting his trademark sparkling smile. The St. Francis Hotel management, it seemed, was honoring one of its own by celebrating the fiftieth employment anniversary of Otis. On that distinctive day, the hotel manager and a clutch of notable guests would gather to celebrate an unlikely hero to so many. At noon, the event commenced.

The manager of the St. Francis spoke first, followed by an impressive queue of other eloquent well-wishers. They conveyed kind words and recounted moments shared with the ever-cheery Otis. The climactic moment came when Otis stepped up to the lectern to say a few words. Looking back on that extraordinary day, I remember that halting but sincere speech; Otis was clearly more adept at one-on-one chats with a dirtied strip of cloth clutched in each hand. As the event ended, the lectern and flowers went back to their designated spots. People dispersed. Soon, the lobby returned to its normal hum of hotel guests and shoppers.

Stepping from my office the following day, I sauntered down the hall toward the men's salon, rounded a corner, and nearly collided with Otis. We both chuckled a friendly greeting and then strolled in tandem, intent on our respective tasks. Walking beside Otis, I sensed in him an inner secret, an amazing answer to things unknown that I needed to discover. It was an odd moment, and looking at him, I sensed he knew what I was thinking.

"Nice little party they threw for you yesterday, eh, Otis?"

"It sure was; yes, indeed, it sure was."

Gazing into his wizened face, I said, "May I ask you something?"

"Go right ahead, Jeff," he replied.

"You're probably the happiest man I've ever met. I mean, you're always in a good mood. You and I have known each other for the past five years, and I truly cherish our friendship, but something just keeps nagging at me. I need to ask you, Otis, but how do you do it? How do you stay so cheerful?"

Then, abandoning the diplomacy I had tried carefully to maintain for so many years, I blurted out the obvious, "I mean, you've worked in the men's salon shining shoes for the past fifty years, and you're still the happiest man I know. How do you do it?"

A smile welled up from deep within his barreled chest. His eyes sparkled, and focusing on some faraway object, he replied with his normally powerful voice now low and steady, "It's really very easy, Jeff. You see, I never just put a shine on a man's shoes; I put a shine on his day."

I've never forgotten those incredible words. It certainly got me thinking about my own approach to selling, and, more importantly, to life. On that day, I realized the sales arena provides amazing communication opportunities with clients. Enhanced communication, it turns out, possesses great power to benefit the customer far beyond the sale. Furthermore, when I choose to do so, I can improve the quality of people's lives by tapping into this power. Otis could not know this as he spoke on that day, but he'd permanently shifted how I saw the selling paradigm and redirected my focus from moving products to "moving" people. Carefully crafted words both transform a client's decision to buy and transform life experiences.

So, how about you? Are you just shining your customer's shoes, or are you creating something greater—a real sparkle?

I know that when I remember Otis, the answer becomes quite clear, my step is a little lighter, and the task at hand is a little easier. Stop shining the shoes, Otis would remind us. It's all about putting … a shine on their day.

Chapter Eight

WARM MONEY SALES

Barely nineteen years old, his youthful face pockmarked with the remnants of acne, the GI dug into the front pocket of his air force-issued coveralls and withdrew a wad of rumpled bills. The wrinkled money now atop the glass jewelry case, he'd made his decision about the engagement ring I had been showing him. He was unsure, however, whether his girl back home would accept the long-distance surprise. For now, he was only certain about the next step.

As I finished putting away the rings he'd considered and then eliminated as "not quite right," all that remained on the glass was the solitary yellow gold ring, its dainty diamond poised in a four-prong setting, and the young man's cash.

Picking up the ring, I felt the chill of its shiny gold shank. With my other hand I swept up the cash, which was warm. Not just warm, but still moist as well. The cool ring was a lifeless object that only its young recipient could animate as she slid it on her finger. The wad of cash, on the other hand, seemed to be almost pulsing from its time stuffed deep in the young man's front pocket during his long quest for the perfect engagement ring.

I was holding, he'd told me, his life savings—two hundred forty-five dollars, precious tender offered up in exchange for … hope and the promise that budding love would withstand the temptations, pain, and trials of great distance. This humble ring on a delicate hand would become the manifest reminder of a kindred heart beating thousands of miles away. All these thoughts flashed through my mind in a split second. Yes, this was the trade: warm money for a symbol.

Early the next morning, as promised, I carefully boxed the ring and wrapped and taped the package for its long journey. At that same moment, I pictured the young man, saddled with gear, climbing aboard the U.S. Air Force plane. This was 1973, which meant destination Vietnam, and his destiny wholly uncertain.

Some days later, I received the return request receipt from the U.S. post office, a barely legible scribble confirming delivery. I could only wonder what had transpired. Did she accept his gift? Were they making plans to marry? Would the young GI ever return home from Vietnam?

To this day, I do not know the answers to these questions. What I do know, and what I have cherished ever since, is that there is value in every sale. There is value in being connected with a fellow human being, even if only for a brief moment. To this day, it is the human contact I find in my chosen profession that remains my most valued treasure. It has always been an honor, especially in the jewelry industry, to be involved in these intimate moments in people's lives.

In our electronic world in this new century, it is indeed rare that a client pulls out a wad of warm cash. And in retrospect, those early "warm money sales" were generally smaller amounts. Since then and throughout my career, I have made much larger sales. But through it all—as I swipe card after card with sixteen-digit numbers and magnetic stripes through an electronic reader—rarely does a day pass that I don't recall my young GI and his pocketful of warm, legal tender. He changed the way I view my role in the selling process.

Ultimately, sales is a role of honor and trust granted to me by my clients. In return, I try to offer kindness and compassion. With that intimate but fleeting bond established, I strive to serve each client with the same reverence I'd give a young man forking over his last dollars.

Chapter Nine

SCOUTING, TRIGGERS & ACTIVATION

Imprisoned by the daily commute, I was being held hostage in my car. Fortuitously, at that moment I sat idling at a most scenic patch along my drive, as the Pacific Ocean twinkled like billions of scattered diamonds atop a massive, royal blue fabric. Gazing out to sea, two distinctly different sounds competed for my attention: the meditative rhythm of crashing waves celebrating their inevitable encounter with land, and a caustic advertisement on my radio belting out nonstop babble. My arm moved unconsciously, and my hand gripped the small, black radio knob. Just as I was about to silence the beast, however, the radio announcer struck something in my memory.

"Bruce Wheeler," I said aloud. A customer of mine from work, Bruce Wheeler, was the man behind the incessant ramble. Quickly I switched courses and cranked the volume up. "Saturday night come to the

Watsonville Fairgrounds for the most spectacular, sensational, exciting auto race of the year. All the top drivers will be there: Roy the Madman Miller, Crazy Chuck Cooper, and, of course, the Maniacal Macho Man of Martinez, Manny Marcos. Be there as they battle it out for the Watsonville Cup. Screaming tires, flying sparks, chest pounding rumbles; you will feel the modified engines burn up the track."

The advertisement jolted me out of the serene seashore scene, and my mind shifted to an image of Bruce Wheeler. He was a great customer and the kind of guy everyone in the store liked. But the image forming in my mind did not match the powerful voice—five foot nothing, blond hair, pale skin, and, most amazingly, a very soft-spoken man. I envisioned other commuters hearing the same advertisement and imagining a Bruce Wheeler who stood seven feet tall and breathed fire.

Just then a horn blasted; traffic had begun to move, but I hadn't. I was soon driving again and wondering what in that radio advertisement gave Bruce's voice such power and dramatic effect. Engines roaring, tires screeching, crowd cheering; the power portion of the commercial clearly jumped out. What had Bruce said and how had he said it that made the commercial so gripping?

I was trying to translate the power of what I'd just heard to the sales arena. Then again, I couldn't exactly create the sound of cheering crowds and burning rubber in my store to sell diamond rings or, better yet, make my voice sound like a circus announcer after too many cups of coffee. What about isolating the universal elements of this message? Perhaps elements extracted from this radio commercial might help with the sales process.

Then something key occurred to me: how effective would the radio spot have been if Bruce described the race literally, that is, a straight description without embellishing adjectives? Such an advertisement for a car race might have sounded something more like this: "Ladies and gentlemen, this Saturday night get your families together, pile into your cars, and make the long drive out to the Watsonville Fairgrounds, where you will likely have difficulty finding a parking spot. The walk to the track will be long and muddy since the grounds are unpaved.

"At precisely 8:00 p.m., we will have a collection of colored cars all lined up behind a white line painted across a section of a large, round asphalt road. As you and your loved ones sit there shivering, since the average nighttime temperature at the Watsonville Fairgrounds hovers in the high forties, we will fire a gun. The cars will then begin to drive around the circular road as fast as they can and proceed in that manner for a full five hundred laps.

"Although you and your family will be able to count the cars as they snap past, after several laps it will be impossible to discern who's leading and which cars have been lapped. Won't that be exciting?"

But Bruce never mentioned the round asphalt road, the painted white line, or even the cars driving around and around in circles. He never gave his audience any literal information. Instead, his words were packed with visual triggers about emotion! He *promised me* that I would feel the rumble in my chest from the super-modified engines. He promised flying sparks and screeching tires. That's the stuff we want!

I would never be interested in packing up my family, driving out to the fairgrounds, fighting for a parking spot, finding a seat on some ice-cold wooden bleacher, huddling together to maintain body heat, and watching cars drive around in circles for hours. If I wanted to watch a bunch of cars drive by, I would take my beach chair down to the freeway.

I knew, however, on Saturday night crowds of people—the faithful aficionados who enjoyed auto races—would flock to the fairgrounds, ignited by these power-packed words brimming with emotion and triggering mental imagery. Those were the elements that would move people from their homes. Imagery and emotion would draw them out to the fairgrounds in droves. These ingredients activate words, make words come alive, and give words sizzle and pop. To ignore imagery and emotion is to leave words flat, linear, and lifeless, i.e., watching cars go around in circles from a cold bleacher. Words turn heads; emotion moves people.

In sales, the right words come alive in a customer's mind. The old adage "sell the sizzle, not the steak" is about focusing on imagery and emotion rather than your product. Let's break this process down into three steps— scouting, triggers, and activation—and take a look at how you can put it all together.

Scouting

Scouting is a search and an analysis of your client's dress, words, and actions that reveals important details about his or her wants, needs, hobbies, and habits. This is not to be confused with assessing your customer, which is attempting to evaluate whether or not your customer is qualified (able, willing, and authorized) to make a purchase. Scouting is about collecting data, understanding your client, and discovering your customer's motivational triggers. A vegetarian's triggers, for example, would not be activated by the sizzle of a steak. Your scouting would reveal such a detail and point you towards a different selling path.

What should we scout for as we work with our customer? The answer: anything—anything that might reveal clues about our customer's likes and dislikes, tastes, or hobbies. Is the customer wearing a golf shirt? If so, consider taking a "golf" direction:

> Well, Mr. Smith, I am sure there are people who think all golf clubs are the same, correct? But you know that there are great differences in the performance of golf clubs, even though they all appear similar. Differences in fine watches are very much the same …

By scouting and then recognizing that your customer enjoys golf, you are able to speak his language on his terms. You explain your product in a language your client recognizes and communicate complicated comparisons within a subject area he knows. In other words, you speak to your customer in shorthand. Shorthand is the method I refer to when I have identified a trait in my client and then shift my language to his language, whether the client is a businessperson, carpenter, executive, nurse, doctor, or banker.

Now, what if you could sell your customer something she already owns? Something she has already decided to purchase and enjoys, something she already loves? That would be a relatively easy sale to make, yes? Through scouting you are able to do just that. Following is another example.

One of the biggest fears customers face in making purchases is the fear of making a hasty decision, i.e., the fear of making a big mistake. Even after they have completed all of their research and done all of the comparison shopping, the decision still requires the exchange of a considerable amount of money. This is normal shopping apprehension. So how do you, as a salesperson, push them into finally making the decision to buy? Well, you don't! Instead, you use scouting to simply sell them something they already own.

Here's how that might look: Your customer is shopping in a jewelry store, viewing a new watch collection. As she views each watch, you observe through scouting that she is wearing round earrings, and the diamond wedding ring she is wearing is round as well. Obviously she seems to favor a round shape over square or rectangle versions. Rather than selling her a new watch with her feeling the risk that she might be making a risky decision, simply remove the sales pressure.

> Mrs. Smith, you seem to favor the round-style watch, which is very comforting. I'll tell you why. At Jones Jewelers, we are trained to make sure that each timepiece fits the owner's lifestyle. We are trained to look for key signs to make sure this happens. I noticed immediately that are you wearing a beautiful round diamond ring, and that your diamond earrings are round as well.

This is exactly what we like to see, because if you were attracted to one of our square watches and purchased it today, you might return to the store in a week or so to exchange it because it really doesn't fit your look. That's because even though a square watch caught your eye, the round shape already looks fantastic on you, plus you already know that you successfully wear the round shape.

Round is a softer, more poetic shape and definitely fits your lifestyle. Take the round watch, Mrs. Smith; it goes perfectly with what you already own.

Instead of focusing all of her attention on the new watch, you remind her (for a moment she relives the purchase in her mind) and resell her on the wise, successful choices she has made in the past coupled with how perfectly this new watch fits into her existing jewelry collection. You sell her something that she already owns.

Through scouting, you increase your chances of making additional sales. You also prevent customers from making hasty purchases because of a spur-of-the-moment impulse. By employing scouting, you are able to match the proper product to the proper customer.

Triggers and activation

You cannot impose your willpower on your customer because this creates sales resistance. You can, however, ignite power within your customer. Only when you tap the power and ignite it within your customer will he or she become activated enough to move from a position of collecting product information to that of making a purchase; it's the law of cause and effect.

Triggers are those bits of information about the customer that you gather and observe through scouting or that your customer broadcasts to you during your conversation. Once you discover these triggers, you can tap into their latent power. When you pull or activate triggers, you will see a clear answer as how to best move your customer closer to a decision. In so doing, your words possess true power and influence because they trigger the pent-up emotional power residing within the customer. This truly is the path of least resistance.

Putting it all together

While I was showing an engagement ring to a young man in my jewelry store one day, he commented, "I have worked in my dad's business since I got out of high school. Unlike my brother."

"What does your brother do?" I asked.

"Basically nothing; he just surfs all the time. He never works."

That was the scouting. Now, how might we tap and activate this customer's key trigger? One option would be to inform him that the diamond he was viewing was graded by the Gemological Institute as a certified G/Vs1, which is actually relevant and extremely important technical diamond information. Or, I could inform him that our credit department offered a ninety-day, no interest plan. What about offering a testimonial of our company's outstanding seventy-five-year history of dependability and outstanding customer service? Describing the facts about the diamond and our store and its colorful history would be much like describing the literal car race on the radio advertisement—cars driving around in circles. Not very exciting or compelling. That method of selling would have little, if any, emotional effect on this customer. Why? Because my customer provided me with a path to his deeper motivational triggers.

He already revealed that he viewed himself as the "good" brother because of his work ethic in the family business. While he'd been working hard for the past few years, his "bad" brother had been playing. So this might prove a more effective response:

> Mr. Customer, the fact that you have chosen to work hard and help build your family business is exactly why you should present a beautiful diamond like this to your fiancée. A diamond of this quality cannot be purchased by just anybody; it is expensive because it is rare, it is beautiful, and it is a symbol of true love. A symbol for all the world to see that someone paid the price to give the very best to the woman he loves.

By activating your customer's motivational triggers, you tap into the power that is most important to them. Thus, you allow them to decide to make a purchase. This lies at the very core of selling. You meet less sales resistance in this way since you are activating a response from your customer rather than pushing for one. The client's decision to buy should always stem from deep within and be generated by internal power, not external (the salesperson). Developing our scouting ability to pick up on verbal and nonverbal clues from our clients will open the door to our customers' true motivations and desires.

In each case, make your sales presentation progress from describing the product in general terms to specific terms related to the client's interests, passions, and profession. This process allows you to quickly grasp the selling points. An added benefit to this technique is the ease in which your client (who may have never known the vast differences in your product) will quickly comprehend and communicate with you on this new subject. By converting your presentation to his language, your client quickly feels more confident because he is well grounded in his language and its terminology. You have tailored a personal sales presentation just for him.

So, a quick review …

Scouting

First: scouting captures important information about your customer through observing both verbal and nonverbal signals. You scout for triggers. Second: scouting informs you which language to speak as you make your presentation.

Triggers

Triggers are your customer's inner buying motivations, which you discover through scouting. "Tapping" triggers is the process of converting those same motivations into the emotional fuel required to make a sale.

Activation

Activation is about creating action and mental movement within your customer. Just because your customer might possess pent-up emotions, in order for him to buy, his motivation must still be activated. You activate it by employing vivid stories throughout your sales presentation, sprinkling in facts and emotion while tapping into his latent buying motives. Use your ability to scout, tap, and activate!

Chapter Ten

(E)MOTION

Goliath Man towered over the group, whip in hand and pacing back and forth along the line, anxious to administer his wrath to anyone who broke ranks or buckled under the horrific strain. Grunting and groaning, the small band of slaves strained under the sweltering heat, tugging desperately at the heavy ropes tethered to a massive stone. Faces contorted, hands blistered and bloodied, their leg muscles bulged like taut bundles of bound steel.

These vivid images flashed before my nine-year-old brain as I, seated alone in the front row of a 1959 movie theater, shoveled handfuls of popcorn into my mouth. I was mesmerized by what I was witnessing up on the screen, and those images played over and over again for years in the miniature movie theater in my head. There's no way I could have known then that Goliath Man would provide enormous insight into my communication skills and sales career.

Years later, while I was conducting a sales seminar in Portland, Oregon, an audience member posed a common question: "How can you get a customer to make a decision?" From fielding this question during seminars numerous times before, I'd learned to slightly modify it to, "How do we get a customer to move to a decision?"

This simple word change—from "make" to "move"—triggered the image of those poor souls struggling to *move* the ridiculously unwieldy stone. The task of building a pyramid should have been impossible without the benefit of large equipment. From just pure brute strength, it simply could not be accomplished!

However, all these years later, the more I ran the movie projector in my mind, the more I began to recall a brief moment in the scene that I had almost completely overlooked. An elderly man wrapped in robes was placing something in front of the large stone the workers were struggling against, something that made their task at least possible: small logs! Obviously, these carefully placed logs reduced the amount of friction the slaves had to overcome.

Suddenly, the concept of creating mental motion in my customers' minds began to fascinate me. After all, this was just a different application of the same sound principles based on physics. Except in this case, the small logs would be carefully placed sales techniques to keep things moving along (even if slowly at times).

The law of inertia states: a body in motion stays in motion, while a body at rest stays at rest. Who amongst us hasn't experienced this law in sales, i.e., a customer who just sits there! It is similar to a 1946 Plymouth I had as a teenager, bought for seventy-five dollars cash: on those occasions when it ran short on gas (which it often did), sputtered to a stop and required a heave to get it safely to the side of the road, moving that beast was like attempting to push a bank. And one with large gold reserves! Definitely a body at rest. Conversely, getting that behemoth steaming down the thoroughfare was the definition of a body in motion. Like watching *Goliath Man*, my seventy-five-dollar car taught me two valuable life lessons:

- It is difficult to get something moving.
- It is easier to keep something moving.

These rules apply to most anything in life. If you've ever tried to get a teenager moving to clean his or her bedroom, you know firsthand about the law of inertia. Conversely, once the room is clean, it's relatively easy to keep it that way. Or, how about dieting and exercising as an adult? We've all been there, but it's a whole lot more difficult to get to the gym and get started than to stay in shape once you're there.

As salespeople, we can tap into this natural law and generate a sort of law of retail inertia. Imagine the sales process as a means of generating mental motion. By applying the proper blend of facts and emotion, we can move a customer from "I'm just looking" to "I'd like that one in red."

As salespeople, we are in the people-moving business; our primary responsibility is to set our customer's mind into motion. The first thing we encounter when attempting to move something, however, is resistance. For years, I saw sales resistance as a customer's negative reaction to my sales presentation, which created a lot of anxiety and frustration in me. Eventually, however, I began to view sales resistance as merely sales friction. Sales friction, much like gravity, is neither positive nor negative—rather it is a natural force we can learn to accept and circumnavigate. This view took the emotional sting out of the equation.

Now, once you're emotionally neutral to client objections, you can remain upbeat and move straight through those objections as just normal sales friction. You just have to learn how, when, and where to keep placing those small logs.

One of the quickest, easiest, and most effective ways to reduce that friction is to switch on your customer's emotions. We've been talking about motion and movement, which we can see is one letter away from what we need to generate in our clients: (e)motion. No emotion, no motion. Or, emotion is motion. That's when the nine-year-old in me popped up again with some great advice: take your customers to the movies. *Goliath Man*!

Rather than exhausting yourself and your customer while searching for just the right words to convince them to make a purchase, try this instead: just help them pull open the curtains on their own miniature movie theater. We all possess one inside our heads. You've probably heard the phrase, "Show them—don't tell them." That means your job is to show your clients a mental movie of a successful purchase, and they'll supply the emotion, generate the mental motion, and move to the point of making their own decision.

Here's how it works: Let's imagine you are showing a client a beautiful engagement ring. No need to go on and on and on about how beautiful the ring is and how much the recipient is going to love and cherish it. Instead, take your customer to the movies. Show, don't tell. Here's how that might sound:

> Mr. Jones, it's interesting, but I had a gentleman much like you in here the other day, looking at an engagement ring as well. However, he was really unsure if his fiancée would like the ring he selected. If I had to say so, he seemed petrified to make the decision. But in the end he did, and out he went with the ring packaged in silver paper with a white satin bow placed on top.

The very next day, two young women burst through the front door of our salon. The tall one began by announcing that she had just gotten engaged. Her fiancée had taken her out to a fabulous dinner and presented her with the most beautiful of engagement rings! Then she told me something I will never forget. She said, "You know, I'll never see the rings my man didn't buy me, I'll only see the one he did." She ended with, "Isn't it beautiful?"

So far in this example, I hadn't told him much about the diamond's features. Instead, I *showed* this uncertain client an even more uncertain client. I helped him start the movie in his head. Then I *showed* him that although the other client felt even less confident than he did in making a decision, this other client went ahead with the purchase. Then, in my client's movie, he ran the scene in the restaurant (with my direction: *action!*) and watched the other client presenting the ring to his fiancée.

Forecasting

Forecasting an image is implanting in your client's mind an image of the positive results your client should experience from making a purchase. In this way, your client will be able to see for himself the good things that will happen from purchasing the ring. When your customer sees himself in the picture, it should stir his feelings of emotion, and those feelings are the powerful fuel needed to propel him into action.

Note: Once you have forecasted to your client a positive image showing success after he has made the decision to buy, *listen carefully to his questions.* The *type* of questions he asks is more important than the question itself.

> Salesperson: Picture your fiancée, Mr. Jones, leaning forward under the glow of a candlelit dinner as you present her with a small, velvet ring box while every head in the restaurant turns to sneak a peek. How exciting it will be for you to witness the look on her face as this beautiful diamond is unveiled. I promise you at that moment this ring you're holding in your hand right now will be the most beautiful ring she has ever seen. That's because it is the ring you gave to her. That's what's most important.
> Customer: What if the ring doesn't fit her finger?

He's made the decision to buy, and this type of question reveals his concern about what could go wrong *after* the sale. Congratulations; you've just elicited a "telltale" question.

Telltales

Throughout history, mariners relied on telltales to gauge the direction and strength of the wind and assure a successful voyage. Telltales were small strips of loose line attached to the sails which enabled the helmsman to assess the wind in detailed ways in order to set the ship's course. Likewise, in selling, the type of questions your client poses are telltales revealing his mental direction, which you can read and assess.

Whenever questions from your client change from inquiries about the product to inquires related to *ownership* of the product (as in the above example), this is a telltale question. Here are some samples of product-driven questions versus ownership-driven (telltale) questions:

Product-driven questions

- Are your prices competitive?
- What other engagement ring styles do you carry?
- Do you guarantee the quality of this diamond?

Ownership-driven (telltale) questions

- If this ring doesn't fit her finger, can we resize the ring?
- What if she prefers white gold instead of yellow gold?
- What if she doesn't like this style? Can she exchange this ring for another design?

Forecasting is my preferred method of prompting a telltale question. Telltale questions from your client help to guide you in the direction that your customer's mind is heading, revealing to you that he has "gone to the movies" and has begun imagining the presentation of the ring to his fiancée and its proper fit.

Close on telltales

Just as a helmsman sets the course by reading the telltales on his sails, you set the course of your sales presentation by telltale questions. The moment you hear a telltale question from your customer (a question of ownership), ask for the sale. Below are two examples. The first shows an attempt to close on a *product-driven* question, while the second uses a telltale or *ownership question.*

Product question:

> Customer: Do you guarantee the quality of this diamond?
> Salesperson: We do. Our store is known for carrying only the very best diamonds. Do you think she would like this one?
> Customer: I'm really not sure. I just started looking. What else do you have?

Ownership (telltale) question:

> Customer: What if this ring doesn't fit her finger? Do you have one in her size?
> Salesperson: Great question. Just present this ring to her, and if it requires any adjustment, you can bring her to

our store, and we will take care of that right here in our shop. That way, she will be wearing the original ring you presented to her. Would you like to have it gift wrapped while I explain your diamond certification papers to you?

Forecasting is a wonderful and creative way of easing your customer's natural decision-making resistance through visualization while at the same time prompting ownership or telltale questions. Your job is simply to buy the tickets and popcorn. *Take your customers to the movies.*

Chapter Eleven

A BOWL OF CINNAMON:
THE ART OF INFORMATION DISTRIBUTION

In 1984, I managed a luxury jewelry store in Washington DC catering to the wealthy and powerful clientele of our nation's capital and the surrounding area. Because of the affluent level of our clients, it was incumbent on me to hire only extremely qualified sales associates for our store. One such applicant approached me with an impressive resume filled with very strong qualifications. As our establishment—well-known throughout the surrounding metropolitan area as the very location to acquire exquisite and expensive diamond jewelry—required knowledgeable salespersons, I was rather awed by this applicant's product information. He had graduated from the Gemological Institute of America, the most prestigious school of its kind in the world. He seemed to know everything there was to know about gemstones, and then some. After two lengthy interviews, I hired him.

Upon completion of our mandatory training on store policy and procedures, which he breezed through with ease, my new sales associate took a post at our diamond counter, which held the most impressive, rare, and expensive collections in our store. I was convinced that with his impressive volume of product knowledge, he was a sure bet for becoming the store's top diamond sales associate.

Eager to see this rising young star in action, I stood off to the side during his maiden diamond presentation—not too close as to be a distraction, but within earshot. The good fortune on this occasion was he had a very striking couple seated before him at the diamond counter. The woman looked elegant in a black St. John suit, had an impressive strand of South Sea pearls around her neck, and wore a diamond Rolex. The man, in a dark blue Ermenegildo Zegna suit with onyx cufflinks, wore a Rolex watch that matched hers.

Never judge a book by its cover, but in this case it was obvious these were our target customers. They were the very reason our store existed, and, best of all, they were sitting in front of my most knowledgeable sales associate. I was sure all three of us were about to experience a dynamic, informative, and powerful diamond presentation.

As my star salesperson began talking, however, I found myself nearly falling asleep. His delivery was packed with data, but it lacked any human element or spark. The entire effect was that of an aged college professor who knows he's the smartest person in the room and is on a mission to prove it. The associate gave a textbook recital on diamonds, their history, and a cold, clinical list of facts on what separated them from all other gems. His presentation was full of too many facts disseminated too rapidly. These poor people were choking on product knowledge as he plowed ahead, unfazed. As soon as they saw the first opening, the clients stood and excused themselves from the store. My new associate seemed perplexed. As he slowly returned the diamond rings to their respective ring trays, I approached him.

"How do you feel that went?" I asked.

"I don't know," he said. "I don't think they were really serious about buying a diamond today."

"Really?" I asked, looking him in the eyes. "Seemed to me they found some time in their busy schedule to do just that."

He continued to put away the diamond rings without looking up. Then I asked, "What were their names?" He looked at me as if I'd just asked him to recite all fifty of the USA's state capitals. I asked another question: "When are they getting engaged?"

Again, the blank stare. I'd made my point, but I wasn't certain he'd fully absorbed the deeper meaning. Regardless, there was no reason to make the guy feel worse than he already did. Either he was going to get it, or he wasn't. So I said, "When you get finished, let's go get some coffee."

Later, as we sat in a nearby coffee shop, we went over his entire sales presentation from the moment his customers entered the store until they left. He shared with me how he had devoted his life to building up his diamond product knowledge. He continued on about how he felt he could become an outstanding salesperson if his customers believed he had superior knowledge. He believed that in most sales situations, his customers rushed him because there was so much product information for them to make the best-informed decision.

As he spoke, I could feel his passion for his customer. He really believed that by having the most product knowledge, he was the best-suited salesperson to help his customers. I needed a way to translate to him, however, that we need a balance of facts and emotion to be successful.

As I sat with this salesperson, I really felt his pain. He was still talking, but I was now searching for a way to help him, some analogy to communicate what he needed to do. And while I was about to find such an example, it turned out to be too late to help my new hire. Just a few weeks later, my new associate quit. Not because he didn't land a six-figure sale right out of the gates, but because he wasn't able to sell anything at all! Even as I tried to tutor him and explain otherwise, he plowed ahead with the belief that having more product knowledge than any other salesperson in the store guaranteed sales. Every customer who came in got scoopful after scoopful of product knowledge shoved down their throats until they ran out gagging. Clearly, the approach was not working.

Back at the coffee-shop break, our first and last together, as it would turn out, he said something to me, but I didn't hear a word, for I was watching a young lady in the far corner of the coffee shop sprinkling something onto her whipped coffee drink—cinnamon. Not too much or too fast, but just enough to complement and enhance her enjoyment. Too much would ruin the whole thing, but in balance, nothing tastes better.

The art of information distribution

Imagine a white bowl heaped with a mound of cinnamon, and then imagine how sick you'd be after eating the entire thing. That is, if you managed to get down the full pile. Conversely, imagine enjoying a warm, flaky, buttered croissant with just a sprinkle of cinnamon.

For our purposes, that bowl of cinnamon represents all of your product knowledge. The way you dispense your product knowledge to your clients can overload them and make them sick, or it can be very pleasant and enjoyable. It isn't the cinnamon itself; it's how you serve it up.

As professional salespeople, we continually need to increase our reservoir of product knowledge, i.e., our own bowl of cinnamon. Providing product information to our clients properly enables them to weigh features and benefits and factor in other elements. Thus, they can make well-informed decisions toward purchasing our product.

Let's compare two sales associates who have the same product knowledge and information, the same inventory, and the same working environment. Now, how is it that two professionals with the same basic tools produce two sets of remarkably different selling results?

The answer takes us back to our bowl of cinnamon—the art of information distribution. The manner in which we offer product education to our clients makes all the difference within the selling process. As professional sales associates, we know on some level that simply spewing product facts is not enough. Today, like never before, our customers are drowning under waves of product data, visual and audio advertising, and internet information. If our success as salespeople was based solely on providing product data to our clients, all sales associates would be as obsolete today as the steam engine and the rotary phone. Again, that's why the art of information distribution holds the key.

Literally speaking, the art of information distribution is the art of dispensing the proper product information during the sales process at the right cadence by being sensitive to each client's natural buying tempo. When building a house, you first begin with a simple foundation, then a framework to support things, and then gradually move to more elaborate materials. Product information, therefore, is best offered in simple terms at the beginning of a sale. You can't slap on a heavy, tile roof before you've built the necessary base and structure. In the early stages, personal connection is the most important element. Then, as your structure grows and is capable of supporting more, you can begin adding more facts about your product as the conversation moves along. Keep your initial bits of product information in client-friendly doses.

As the salesperson, you must be attuned to your client's responses and reactions to additional information. Then you can carefully adjust your pace and tempo of delivering product information. In the end, the amount of product information you distribute to the customer is entirely based on the customer's response to receiving that information, not your personal agenda or requirement to provide everything you know.

Ask any architect, engineer, or contractor what happens when you break the natural sequence of building a structure. Disastrous results! By layering product information into the sale using a suitable sequence, however, you build your client's interest, desire, and motivation to purchase your product. The client, through appropriate increments of product information, more clearly comes to realize that the product will add to his or her quality of life. In that way, the process becomes a delicate dance between salesperson and client, where you sprinkle product information throughout the sale at a pace that keeps the client in control. All you need to do is actively follow your client's lead. I've watched firsthand what can happen when salespeople don't.

Chapter Twelve

COSMIC CON

"Daddy, the moon is chasing our car!"

As the family station wagon hurtled down a West Texas highway, the young child gazed into the black cosmos from the back window. Hypnotized by the platinum orb he was certain was in pursuit, he awaited his father's response to this imminent peril.

And I, his father—stiffened hands gripping the steering wheel, exhausted wife curled up in the passenger seat in slumber—whispered in response, "No, son. The moon is not really chasing our car." I paused, choosing the simple answer. "It just appears to be chasing us. The moon never moves."

"But it is moving," my son persisted. "It's moving above the tree tops. It's following us; I'm watching it, Dad!"

Reluctantly, I pulled my gaze from the hypnotic tunnel of oncoming headlights and leaned out to look into the star-saturated sky. Sure enough, there was the moon, racing above blackened tangles of branches like an engorged firefly. A small smile began to emerge across my face as I recalled the first time, as a small child, I'd determined the same thing. *He's right,* I thought to myself, *the moon is following us.*

"First of all ..." I cleared my throat in preparation for the eloquent and detailed answer to my son's observation, which might include discussions of the earth's rotation and the parallax principle. But even as I began this insightful treatise, my young audience had fallen to sleep, oblivious to the droning genius that was to follow. Neither a child's misconception that the moon is following him, nor an adult's that their past is following them are correct; both are based on perception rather than reality.

In reality, our mistakes, regrets, failures, and setbacks are suspended in time, bound to the very moment they occurred. Incapable of time travel, such travails are not following us! It is only when we choose to cling to them, relive them forever, and untie and retie them in a way that puts us at rest that we drag them forward to pollute the present.

And this is the great "cosmic con," because it is only through our breath of life that we continue to feed power into our past. Without such continuous nurture of thought and attention, our baggage would simply wither away and disappear.

As I was about to explain to my son that night, what we call "moonlight" is actually only a reflection of the sun's light. In the same way, our mistakes and regrets are merely a reflection of the power we continue to project onto them. Assume this challenge: Just for today, release your mistakes, regrets, and any setbacks you're keeping alive. Stop feeding them with thought, energy, and emotion. Assume the courage to turn away from them. Starve them of any further power. Open your clenched fist and let them spill away like sand through your fingers.

Now, doesn't that feel better?

Once you've learned the lesson from any mistake, all that's left is to let the mistake go. Allow mistakes to retreat in the rearview mirror, growing ever smaller and smaller, and let them stay where they should—in your past! At some point you'll look back, and while they're still back there somewhere, you won't even be able to see them anymore. Just leave them there; no need to make a U-turn, speed back, and bring it all to life again. Keep driving forward.

Now you're free to devote all your power to affecting the present moment, which is all you can control. This is where change, closure, liberation, and enlightenment await. The continuous passage of time will become the solution and salvation to all our pains and regrets. Time will become our healing balm. Time will be the river that carries us away from the moments of our past and into sparkling new moments of the here, now, and beyond. Move along with time at its natural rhythm and tempo; allow the passage of time to sweep you up and carry you into your future. Once again, let go. Release your desperate grasp; stop clinging.

Now, rather than feeling like past misdeeds are chasing you, become an aware passenger in time. Be a silent witness of events, which you traverse, observe, feel, appreciate, and let go. This is how we leave all the old, heavy, dusty baggage behind. You can then remain grounded, knowing that we all make mistakes and all have regrets and things we wish we could do over.

Let time do what was intended for you. Embrace the belief that when you unload all that extra baggage and leave it where it occurred—the past—you free yourself on all levels.

The moon is not following you; it's just reflecting the light and power of the sun. You, too, have that same power to warm, heal, and enlighten. Now the big question: where will you shine your light, and what will you reflect back to yourself?

"Repetition is the spice of life"
J. Cox

Chapter Thirteen

INVISIBLE PEOPLE

I had always imagined I noticed everyone in my life, but fortunately for me, a fifty-nine-dollar, black-and-white security monitor taught me otherwise. I had just pulled my rental car into the Collin Creek Mall parking lot in Plano, Texas, a suburb of Dallas, late one August afternoon. I was dreading stepping out into the stifling heat. As regional sales manager for Black Starr & Frost, a high-end jewelry firm headquartered in Alexandria, Virginia, it was my responsibility to visit our locations across the country and provide merchandising and sales training.

This particular visit, unfortunately, had been prompted by a disappointing company-wide sales report just released at our national sales meeting, and the Collin Creek Mall store sales results were particularly alarming. Although the sales history always pegged this location as a top performer for our firm, that was not the case since the previous store manager's departure and subsequent replacement. In fact, store sales had taken a dramatic downward spiral. Hot, humid weather aside, this was not a celebratory visit.

After countless conversations on the phone with the new manager over the past few weeks, I began to wonder if he was exerting half as much effort in selling to customers as he was in trying to sell me on why his store's sales were so poor! I had my doubts, so instead of continuing our less-than-fruitful conversations over the telephone, I made plans to fly to Dallas and continue our discussions with some quality one-on-one time. Hence, I found myself sitting in the Collin Creek Mall parking lot.

As I climbed from the car, as anticipated, the Texas sun laid siege as I crossed the asphalt lot. Rivulets of perspiration inched between my shoulder blades beneath my dark blue business suit (company policy, Texas or not). Finally, I reached the main mall entrance, pulled open the door, and savored the blast of conditioned arctic air.

Minutes later, I'd located our store. Knowing full well my visit was on the docket, the store was like some real-life diorama of retail sales success. In fact, every salesperson was engaged in conversation and showing merchandise to a customer. *This doesn't help your case much, Mr. New Manager*, I thought to myself as I bypassed the song-and-dance on the sales floor and found the manager's office.

Trimmed in rich wood paneling and featuring an opulent desk and chairs and thick, luxurious carpeting, the manager's office in the salon was most impressive. Designed as a sanctuary for the affluent customer invited in to look at special and rare collections of jewelry and gems, this back room was actually the heart of the store. This was also where I discovered our new manager as I might have imagined him: feet up on desk and chomping potato chips!

My entrance seemed to light a fire, and he sprung to his feet mumbling, "Mr. Cox ..." as bits of greasy chips tumbled from his mouth and fingers. "I didn't think that you would be here so soon." *Should it matter?* I thought. I could only imagine what happened on the days he knew I was thirteen hundred miles away on the East Coast. He grabbed a paper towel and brushed off his mouth and tie, but we both knew he'd missed the opportunity.

"Not much traffic," I said.

And off he went, rambling on and on about how dead the store had been since they'd opened this morning. In his disparaging comments, he took a micro-to-macro approach, starting with the mall, and then followed by choice words for the municipality and the state of Texas. He book-ended nicely by returning to the micro and blaming the lowly customers themselves. I never knew for sure if I heard this or imagined it, but I think he even ended with something bad about his own mother!

I just let him talk. He finally ran out of steam and just stared at me. I started by sharing my sincere concern that he felt his situation was so bad, and that we, as a leadership team, never intended to make things difficult for him. Collectively, I explained, the executive sales team believed the Collin Creek store was a strong location in an affluent Dallas suburb with enormous potential. Based on its past sales performance, this should be an outstanding career opportunity for any ambitious employee.

Then he took his turn, wherein he did his best to convince me that there were no customers left to sell to from this store. He argued that the last manager had sold all the jewelry and watches anyone who lived within a seventy-five-mile radius of the Collin Creek Mall could ever want. He even said, "This store is tapped out! Besides, hardly any customers come in the store for us to work with."

That last comment literally got my ears hot. To appease the onset of boiling frustration, I asked, "Will you please pull the security tape from last Saturday, put it in the VCR, and play it for me?" We both knew it was less a question and more a directive. "But," I quickly added, "set it on fast forward."

Although he didn't seem to see where this was going, he produced the tape and did as I'd asked. We watched in complete silence. The vintage monitor began blinking and then revealed its precious contents on the screen. The black-and-white tape soon showed people buzzing around the store as the fast forward mode made them appear animated.

"Push stop," I commanded.

As he pressed stop, a well-dressed woman appeared in the center of the screen pushing what looked to be a baby stroller.

"Who is she?'" I asked.

"Her …" he replied slowly, "she's a pain. No one wants to work with her. She just wastes your time, she won't buy anything anyway, and she's just taking her baby for a stroll."

I told him to push the start button once again. "Stop," I said after a moment. "Who is he?'"

This time, a man in dress slacks and a dress shirt was frozen on the screen, and he seemed to be standing in front of the watch counter.

"Who is he?" I repeated.

"Him. Forget him—that guy is always in here checking out watches. He'll ask us a million questions, but, like always, he never buys one. Again, he just wastes our time."

We repeated this game, and every time a customer popped up on the monitor and I asked him to stop the tape, he told me some variation of the same story. It was clear to me that people had become invisible to him. At day's end, he and I had a serious discussion on that very subject, and I reminded him of our firm's commitment to providing quality customer service to everyone who entered our salons, whether they made a purchase or not. He knew, too, that he was on thin ice and that we were expecting a turnaround. And he had months, not years, to do so.

During my flight home hours later, I sat gazing out the cool, plastic window at the twinkling lights of cities far below. I was haunted by a question: how many people pass through our lives every day who, for one reason or another, have become invisible to us? It's as if we ignore their very existence. Could it be that if they do not provide value to us, we do not assign value to them?

I determined at that moment, right there in seat D, row 22, that I would change my life immediately and forever. Starting then, and for as long as I was here on Earth, I promised to give my full attention to everyone with whom I came into contact. A stranger, a salesperson, a client, a loved one—I would treat them the same. I would clear my mind and focus solely on them.

In this way, I'd simply refuse to allow anyone to pass through my life unnoticed. By getting outside myself, I was choosing to be in the moment with each person. A lack of customers was not the problem for the new manager of the Collin Creek store. As I'd seen on the tape, they were everywhere. He was drowning in a sea of customers, but they had become invisible to him! The final chapter in that story, by the way, was that I was not able to help my new manager change his ways, and he went on to grouse about all those invisible customers to a new boss at a different company.

As salespeople, when we search for customers, we automatically exclude blocks of people. This happens because most of us generally have a preset customer profile or client template in our mind. This causes us to search for a type of person who has either purchased something from us in the past (I work well with businessmen or women in their fifties) or a type of customer we've seen another salesperson successfully sell (it's easy to sell to women who carry Gucci or Prada handbags).

By commanding your mind to search for this preset customer, you are limiting your vision to only those people. In doing so, you completely miss a parade of potential customers. I have received countless telephone calls from excited salespeople over the years that generally start out the same way: "Jeff, you won't believe what just happened to me. This guy was just walking through the store dressed in a T-shirt and shorts. None of the other salespeople approached him, so I did, and he ended up buying a twenty-thousand-dollar watch!" This opening statement is generally followed up with the other half of this predictable tale.

"And guess what else—he is a company founder, owner, CEO/ heir to X fortune/ prince of island nation/ invented something we use every day/ etc. He told me that the only reason he was in casual clothes today was because he had been working on his yacht/ posing for a GQ shoot/ checking on his racehorse/ taking his new Maserati for a spin/ etc."

Why are these salespeople always so shocked? My theory is that the actual customer, the customer they sold, was of a completely different profile than the customer they envisioned in their brain. Their genuine surprise in saying, "I can't believe he bought something," is confirmation of my theory. Even after thirty-five years in sales, I have fallen into this same trap, especially when I think I desperately need to make a sale (a belief and energy that almost invariably leads to not making a sale).

That little fifty-nine-dollar, black-and-white security monitor taught me an even greater lesson that day in Dallas. It taught me that as much as I thought I noticed the people around me, I, in fact, did not. I determined to develop a heightened awareness of my surroundings in order to distill my focus and enhance my attention toward everyone and everything I encountered.

This enhanced attention developed into an enormous benefit to both my sales career and my wider everyday life. By developing new vision, I began capturing what I'd missed. By continually refreshing my attention level, I discovered a deep sense of peace and joy in life's most mundane routines. And life, as it turns out, includes a lot of mundane routines.

Rather than viewing my daily two-hour commute as the same old routine, I imagine it as a different commute each day. Trees along the highway develop new buds, new blades of grass sprout up, and billowing clouds create a ballet across the heavens; it is, literally, never the same! You can be cynical and say, "That Jeff Cox is on drugs." Or you can loosen your tight grip, return to when you were more innocent, as we all once were, and give it a try. If you're reading this book, I'll bet you're in the latter category.

When we begin searching for those subtle differences and nuances occurring all around us each moment of the day, we begin to feel the beautiful rhythm and texture of it all. We're struck by the gravity of the realization that life is dynamic, constantly changing and evolving, and that mundane, routine life is enough for us! That's right; life is enough. It requires nothing else added for full enjoyment.

I have spent the majority of my life selling the highest level of luxury jewelry from Black Starr & Frost, the oldest fine jewelry firm in America. I've sold for Neiman Marcus, one of the premiere retail establishments around. After thirty-five years of procuring extraordinary gems from all over the globe for the most discerning clientele, I have learned something invaluable: during their final hour, not one of my thousands of customers would ask that their jewelry collection be gathered and displayed around their hospital bed one last time.

I would imagine that in that moment, true beauty might be found in the warmth and brilliance of sunlight pouring through the hospital windows, in the loving, subtle touch of a granddaughter's hand, or in the memory of a special afternoon spent with a spouse, family, and friends. In those fleeting gems of time, I imagine the tone and texture of the human voice might surpass the finest music ever composed. In the end, the answer may rest in the staggering beauty of commonness that eventually grips our soul and reminds us of our humanity.

So it is with a profound sense of responsibility—to my maker and to my fellow humans—that my calling includes and transcends "selling." My larger mission is to share this deep appreciation for the beauty of commonness with you, dear reader. My mission is to see, not make other human beings invisible.

More important than how much we sell is that each one of us develops this special ability for seeing the invisible, noticing the unnoticed, and never missing the hidden beauty bound within all we experience in our daily lives. Ultimately, then, we all might come to realize that mundane repetition is, indeed, the spice of life.

MOMENTS OF DISCOVERY

The most amazing selling method, one that has increased my income and catapulted my career, came to me not as I sat atop a bluff overlooking the sea. Instead, this amazing secret quite literally jumped into my lap. What is the source of this greatest lesson about improving one's sales ability and connecting with customers? An unlikely duo: a six-year-old and a four-year-old.

"Popi, Popi!" they hollered in tandem, "Popi" being my assigned moniker for granddaughters Hurricane and Cyclone. Or as they are denoted by their respective birth certificates: Portia and Chloe. Gone were any lingering hopes of an impromptu nap. My addled brain registered this truth as Portia and Chloe exploded through the red front door, fresh from a *Finding Nemo* matinee. Their mother, my daughter, trailed behind.

As their cherubic faces energized the living room with excitement, their palpable animation engulfed me, an invisible force drawing me upright from the warm creases of the couch. Their enthusiasm burst forth with flailing arms, hops, and facial contortions as they exclaimed, "Popi, there was a baby striped fish named Nemo that talked … sharks, Popi, sharks … There were gigantic sharks!"

As they swept me up into their world—vibrant, enchanting, packed with gobs of colors, vibrations, and emotion—something clicked and a question bubbled forth in my mind: *Why is their communication so attractive, so engaging, and so effective on me?* Suddenly, I needed to answer that question by discovering and defining the underpinnings of this natural method of transmitting information. I'd later dub it the "Sharing vs. Selling" method.

Sharing vs. selling

As salespeople, we have a responsibility to supply basic product facts, features, and benefits to our clients. This information is a vital element of our job, as it assists our clients in making the decision whether to purchase a product.

Our challenge, however, in providing clients with product facts, features, and benefits is to do it without creating sales pressure or sales resistance. Sales resistance is generally the result of our methods of delivering information, not the client's methods of receiving it. Therefore, we must shift our focus to the conversational environment we create in our client's mind during our sales presentation.

We must accept our responsibility for creating an engaging environment where we share our sales story with our clients, invite them into our world, and build up their desire for more product information. That's the inherent, organic form of communication within us all, the one employed by my granddaughters without conscious effort. Quite simply, if everyone is granted this form of communication at birth, then it should be possible for each of us to tap back into its enormous power at will.

Portia and Chloe were not telling me about the movie or selling me on the story; they were sharing their passion.

Passion generates emotional gravity.

When we successfully transmit passion, we can sweep others up into our emotion, draw them into our experience, and make them feel what we feel. Sharing our passion becomes extremely contagious. When we are passionate, we become more engaging, more magnetic, and more convincing. Instinctively, our clients are drawn in by this emotional gravity and begin to experience our passion for themselves.

Imagine clients saying, "Really?" and "Is that so?" and "That's amazing!" Imagine how rewarding it would be for you both to share such a real sense of participation and excitement over your sales presentation.

It can happen. You will begin to hear comments such as these once you convert your sales presentation from the delivery of facts to the sharing of passion. So, how do we do this?

1) Isolate the facts, benefits, and features of your product or service. These are the elements that must impassion you. They are what make your product or service unique. There is an old gospel song that goes, "If you want to be convincing, be convinced!" To be successful in selling, you must first be utterly sold on your product or service. Secondly, you must be convinced that it is the best solution for your customers' needs. Pick two or three elements of your product that make it stand out from your competition, and share these facts with pride and passion.

By the way, don't forget to include the people who make your product. I always mention to my customer the people who manufacture my product. I share with my customer that although they will never meet face to face with the people who build our product, I have, and so I relay the craftspeople's passion and commitment to quality to my client.

2) Share rather than present. Share what you know with a sense of discovery, as if you had just discovered this new information for the first time. In this way, you draw your client into your world rather than push him or her away with a sales pitch. Your message becomes personal, and your customer feels what you are sharing rather than simply hearing your words.

For example, rather than saying, "Our company is the leader in so and so," try sharing this information with a sense of discovery. Say, "We just found out that our company became number one in the industry. It's amazing to me that in just four years the public has voted us number one!" or, "I was surprised to find out that our company is the only one in the field still building each component by hand!"

3) Show your passion. Showing your passion by sharing with a sense of discovery is powerful, persuasive, and potent, and it is less threatening to your client. It is less threatening because you are not attempting to sell them as much as you are sharing with them something that excites you.

We all know customers would rather make a purchase than be "sold." Create a comfortable environment for your client, an environment where he or she feels safe while being informed and entertained. Project an engaging environment where your client is allowed to make a purchase. Remember, this engaging environment is created automatically whenever you share your passion about anything—a fantastic movie, a recent vacation, your exceptional children, or your wonderful product. The reason is because it's a method of communication that draws people *into your message* rather than pushing them away.

Finally, it's your responsibility to properly transmit the information to make your presentations irresistible. All it took for me to grasp this were two little girls, Portia and Chloe, who are not professional public speakers, and nor do they have university degrees or any formal training. They do, however, have the same wonderful quality that's inside you: passion, that magnetic method of communication that's simply enchanting.

Chapter Fifteen

SOFTWARE UPGRADE

When it was time for a new computer, my wife recommended that I buy a PC rather than a Mac. She warned me, correctly, that we didn't know anyone who owned a Mac, so if I ran into problems, we wouldn't know what to do or where to turn for help.

She's right, I thought, and then I went out and bought a Mac anyway. My wife's wisdom aside, I'm so happy I did because it actually taught me the meaning of life. But first, some quick back story ...

A few days into owning and exploring my new toy, I was getting a real feel for it, and, for an old dog (at this writing, I am fifty-five years old), even getting pretty good at how to navigate and use all the bells and whistles. Then, some weeks later, I saw an advertisement on television for a Mac software program called, "Garage Band." The advertisement promised that by installing Garage Band onto your Mac, you could create your very own music.

"I've got to have Garage Band on my computer," I told my wife. The look she returned to me had the same emotional tenor and overall effect as the one I got the day I came home with the Mac in the first place. "Never mind," I said, quietly unplugging my Mac, slinking away, and lugging my cumbersome desktop computer downtown to the Mac store.

After standing in line for almost an hour, my arm had gone numb, but it was finally my turn to speak with the help expert. I began by telling him how much I liked—no, loved, my Mac—and how I was the only one we knew who owned a Mac (all of our friends had PCs), and how I felt that my Mac was one of the finest pieces of human engineering ever unfurled. Then I got to the heart of my mission—the new Garage Band software—and how my very happiness at that moment, and forevermore, depended on having the program installed immediately.

There was a brief pause as the store employee looked at me as if I was Rain Man (minus the math skills), and then he said, "You already have Garage Band, sir. It's been on your hard drive since you got your Mac."

As my face went flush, chuckles emanated from the line of waiting customers behind me. I'd probably laugh at me, too.

"I already have it?" I asked, as if my authoritative tone might restore some measure of belief in my intelligence.

"You do," he replied.

With that, there wasn't much more I could say to salvage the situation. I simply smiled, hoisted my computer into my "live" arm, and went home completely humbled.

Now what does any of this have to do with the meaning of life? Everything. After working with the public for more than thirty-five years, I have had the pleasure of meeting thousands upon thousands of people from all over this great, big, beautiful world of ours. One truth I have discovered: almost without exception, when you talk to people and scratch the surface, you realize we are all searching for the same things—joy, peace, and in the end, happiness.

The various searches people undertake come in different forms, whether constant travel, work, material accumulation and consumption, addictions, partners ... Whatever the method, the goal of the search is always the same. It is this relentless search that reminded me of my own search for the latest software.

The pattern goes like this: First, you hear a buzz about the latest, newest, best thing out there that you absolutely must have. In that instant, some element of your life needs an upgrade—your computer, your chosen partner, your bank account, your body fat percentage, the lines around your eyes, your hair color, your house, your car, your carpet, and on and on—but, and here's step two, don't just sit there. Go on the quest to find true happiness, because here's the solution. But it never seems to be the solution when we find it, at least not a fulfilling or lasting solution.

Which leads us back to my Garage Band software, the final destination and mountaintop of all things glorious, that, well, I had all along. Just as I did that day, I fear most people in this world are on a frantic search for something they already possess. The place you seek is where you are already standing, just like the glasses perched atop your head as you frantically search for them or the car keys safely in your pocket. So, the question becomes: what's the secret to discovering something that you already possess?

Stop looking where it isn't.

Why is it so easy for us to search for happiness "where it isn't"? I think we do so because it's always easier to begin our search outside of ourselves. This point of view places the responsibility for our own happiness outside of us. Rather than claiming the responsibility for creating our own happiness, we become "victims" affected by the events of the cosmos and random happenings. In this distorted state, our focus is fixed on the dynamic and ever-shifting *outside world,* a place we will never control. And yet, we fool ourselves into thinking that somehow … someday … we will. We won't, though. In the end, much like a computer gone haywire, our little hourglass keeps spinning while we are stuck in eternal search mode.

The first awareness needs to be that it's not the external events that will ultimately bring us true happiness, but rather our internal choices and interpretations of whatever is actually happening. Be it new relationships, more money, or mounting material possessions, all external events provide a spike of happiness in the beginning. Eventually, however, we discover all external events and possessions have a shelf life and an expiration date, and whatever momentary pleasure we gained from these objects begins dissolving the moment we attempt to hold onto them.

The truth is whenever we attempt to capture and hold onto these fleeting moments of happiness, we are much like a small child who has imprisoned a beautiful butterfly in a glass jar. The very moment he screws the top onto the jar to protect his beautiful and precious treasure, the fate of the creature is sealed as well.

And so we exist on an emotional roller coaster, completely gripped by the influence of external events. By this path, our happiness only occurs when we deem something good comes our way.

Ending the war of the worlds

We operate concurrently in two worlds—the inner world (our thoughts, reactions, responses, feelings, free will, etc.), and the outer world (random events, situations, and outside occurrences). We also know, logically, that we cannot control the events in our lives (the outer world), only our reactions to or interpretations of those events (the inner world). Let's consider our situation from a brand new vantage point or perspective.

Perspective: your master key

In 1973, I worked for a hotel lodge in Cannon Beach, Oregon. My title was "maintenance man." Translation: *fix whatever's broken.* This mandate required that I have access to every room on the property. The best way to accomplish this with the least amount of effort was to be in charge of a master key to the entire facility. I checked out the master key each morning and returned it at the end of the day.

Imagine—one key that could unlock every door you might encounter as you performed your daily tasks! To carry a separate key for every door would be a ridiculous, time-consuming burden that would require standing in front of each door while fumbling with hundreds of similar keys. And yet, isn't that what we normally do? We look for a different key to unlock every situation.

Instead, whenever you find yourself in a situation wondering which key in your pocket is the correct one to unlock your sense of joy, happiness, or inner peace, remember that you, too, already have a master key for opening every door or situation you will confront in your life. How? It is your inherent ability to adjust your perception of any situation. Your master key is your ability, your power, and your given right to change your perspective about anything. And, yes, this priceless tool was all part of your original software package!

At the beginning, we each received a perfect version of the "happiness software." However, this was not a promise that we will only encounter events that make us happy. Rather, it was a promise that we possess the ability to adjust our perceptions so we might view the same situations differently. Instead of always searching for better, faster, sleeker, and sexier versions to make us happy, all we need to do is look inside and use what we already have. That's where we'll find exactly what we need. It's been right there in your pocket or purse all this time—happiness software, your master key.

Chapter Sixteen

BLACK & WHITE

Visitors to our home are inevitably attracted to the central hallway, where well-arranged photographs adorn the walls—black and whites recording the past. An accomplished shutterbug, my highly creative wife Mary snapped a number of them herself and pulled others from family albums. With the magic of photo software, Mary produced an art gallery texture in each with a gray-scaled hue. The general consensus is that the overall effect works rather well.

As I'm often hurrying to an airport or to see my grandchildren, I rarely stop to appraise and appreciate the significance of those images. When I do finally pause, though the occasion is infrequent, this family-line gallery conjures almost instant contemplation. Its membership, some still living and some having left this sphere long ago, recalls varied lives brimmed with passion and pain, defeat and victory, failure and success. Through this thread of time, I remember my loved ones.

Then my own mortality edges into the proceedings, and I realize that my black and white will one day be on the wall. Someone, perhaps Mary or one of our children, will choose just the right image, settle on an appropriate matte and frame, and position me good and straight amongst all the ancients. From there onward, that one particular photograph—a single image of Grandpa Jeff frozen in time—will smile evermore from its spot in the hallway. I hope they give me a good view.

Often, as I give a presentation and scan the audience, these thoughts reinsert themselves, and I become aware that not only will I, the speaker, become a black-and-white photograph some day, but so, too, will all the listeners staring up at me. It's simply … inevitable. The cycle of life.

Sensitive to any less-than-positive effect on a gathering, I never share these thoughts of quiet acceptance at my speaking engagements. Death and mortality are still largely feared in our culture and certainly rarely, if ever, discussed openly. No matter who we are, however, and regardless of what we have accumulated and accomplished in our lives, ultimately, we all end up as old photos suspended on family walls somewhere. That inescapable reality, for me, becomes a battle cry—now is the time to do our living … right now, more than ever.

Now is the time to hug and kiss our loved ones and squeeze as much warmth as we can into each day. Now is the time to affect each person in our lives, everyone we know and encounter in our daily world, giving them that extra bit of compassion, mercy, and joy. Now is the time to try to go one full minute or hour—a day even—and let go of any resentment, judgment, or condemnation of any other human being. (It's harder than it sounds!)

We do these things because once our lives become black-and-white snapshots, it will be far too late to embrace, encourage, and love those who have marched lockstep with us through life. Were we to hold out hope that one day someone would pass our faded black and white and be filled with fond memories of our time on earth, we'd have missed the message. "Now" is what counts most.

While writing this book, I found myself at odds with the dark theme of mortality and how it might improve one's ability to share, sell, and communicate. Though, the more I fought against and reconsidered its inclusion, the more I grasped its value within the sales arena because sales can only unfold within the larger arena of life.

Appreciation improves interaction between all persons. By being able to truly appreciate our clients, we show that they matter to us. One of the quickest ways to show your appreciation of another human being is by granting them your full and undivided attention. Here are three things I do to demonstrate my full attention to another:

> 1) Completely focus on the person. A good habit is to remind yourself that this meeting is one of a limited number of times you will see each other during your entire lives.

> 2) Provide nonverbal feedback. Reflect your reactions to the person's comments, making sure to include signals that let them know you're engaged in the conversation. Give a nod of the head, a smile, a wince—whatever the appropriate response. Own your responsibility to make sure the other person knows you're engaged.

> 3) Ask a question-continuum. Ask open-ended questions that encourage the other person to continue their story or point. Here are a few examples: "Really, what did you say after she said that to you?"; "How did that make you feel?"; or "So what are your plans now?"

Each person needs to know deep down inside that you see them, hear them, and value them—in essence, that they matter to you. When clients matter to us, we're able to view the sales presentation more through their eyes than only through our own. From this vantage point, our language with buyers becomes transformed and enhanced. Our clients can then feel and enjoy this genuine concern and authentic verbal and kinesthetic communication. Black-and-white worlds of interaction become saturated with dazzling color.

I have no time to squander and no time to pause and consider what photograph of me will end up on the wall. The life I create will dictate what image and essence the camera one day captures. And with that thought, I'm out of the hallway, out the front door, and happily greeting the driver who will take me to the airport while I ponder my next business engagement. Between here and there, I understand, is a whole world of possibility.

"No act of kindness, no matter how small is ever wasted."
Aesop (620 B.C.-560 B.C.)
The Lyon and the Mouse

Chapter Seventeen

THERE GO I

Oily, shiny, haggard, and hairy—those were the four words that popped into my mind to describe a tattered man struggling and straining to will his rusted shopping cart through the crosswalk. He passed directly in front of my gleaming SUV with only a tapestry of soiled rags separating his scarecrow frame from the elements.

His masked face sported a gangly beard of silver straw accented by pitch brown and yellow swaths running its full length. A veteran smoker, I guessed. He appeared to have few teeth, if any. His leathery face caved inwards around his mouth. The once-shiny shopping cart, much like its owner, had been pushed beyond its life expectancy; now both desperately clung to the remaining grains of sand in the hourglass. Then there was the dog, muddling along a few feet in tow. The matted mutt resembled his human in more than gait, a creature seemingly determined to see this saga to its predictable conclusion.

I knew what was about to happen—the traffic light would go green and leave the duo hopelessly stranded in the center of the roadway. My stomach churned, and I thought, *There's no way you're gonna make it across in time. Hurry!* But, unfazed, the disheveled caravan pressed onward. Somehow, those rust-colored forearms and canine paws willed forward the procession and its precarious stack of mismatched cargo. The sum of the man's worldly possessions was piled skyward in black garbage bags—clothing, bedding, parka, utensils, and such. A strange thought came to me, but shouldn't two, possibly three black bags suffice? The man appeared to have fifteen or twenty bags—a huge amount of excess ballast and ongoing hindrance to him and his dog. Why would anyone drag all that unnecessary baggage around? What comfort could it possibly add to the quality of his life? Then again, did he feel comforted by dragging it along with him? The race against the clock continued as they neared the curb. Wheels clacking, paws trotting, bulging black bags bouncing, I quickly stole a glance at the traffic light to my left. The light was yellow—time had all but run out.

Green. Time froze.

Then, as if the Good Lord hit the fast-forward button on the remote control from a celestial La-Z-Boy, all hell broke loose. A cacophony of snarling car and truck horns unleashed a piercing wave of judgment. Vehicles inched forward like preschoolers clamoring toward the playground. The man's teeming baggage coupled with the sheer will it took him to push it across the thoroughfare had cost him once again; he was trapped. He was outnumbered, overwhelmed, and overrun. A painful tithe would be issued to the universe for needing the unneeded. The scene sent a pain through my gut.

It was the black garbage bags that haunted me the most. Why all the bags, why so many? Why drag them along? The idea of him dragging all that useless baggage around seemed simply ridiculous to me. What a waste of energy. Didn't he realize that all his excess baggage was weighing him down? More importantly, how long had he been pushing that overloaded cart around? It was baggage that served no purpose, and yet he could not simply let it go.

Then I realized my judgment was because it was my own shopping cart that was brimming with the past. How would I ever be able to fully experience the present moment if I polluted it with all the refuse I refused to jettison?

"But by the Grace of God, there go I." It was starting to make sense to me. Suddenly, I fully understood just how, and why, I had been stopped at that light at that very moment. Rather than just a homeless man wandering down the road, the man pushing the cart was a man wandering through my life. He had a powerful purpose. He had value.

All I needed to do was be still and see the truth: it was I crossing the street that day. It was I struggling with a cart filled with black plastic garbage bags stacked to the heavens. Every new moment of every day, I, too, was dragging my tired collections of past garbage bags. With friends, with strangers, at work and play; I never left home without them.

Suddenly, I began to see them *everywhere!* Arguments with people in my past ... I hauled those around. Upsets, unfairness, an undeserved grade in school, a thwarted romance ... more black bags. Missed opportunities, comparing my life with others more fortunate, missed promotions ... bags, bags, and more bags. My own cart of overflowing debris was an oil tanker to that man's little rowboat, all of it sorted, arranged, and catalogued so that whenever the situation merited I could pull a bag out and dump it all over the moment. Within a few city blocks, I pulled to the side of the road and shut the engine off. I said a prayer. I asked God to forgive me that day. I asked to be forgiven for missing all the new moments of life he had freely given to me as a gift of his love. I had missed them because of my insecurity and my desire to be right at all costs.

Because of my choice to hold onto negative garbage in my past so that I might convince others of wrongs done to me, I had missed so many glorious, unfolding moments of the present. Just like that homeless man, I, too, was a tattered being with a cart filled with garbage. And just like that, I chose to let it all go.

And yes, I stayed to make sure he made it across the intersection safely. I think of him often and wonder where he is and how it all unfolded. He has no idea of the gift he gave me that day. I will forever be both comforted and inspired by the image of his tired, tattered face.

Chapter Eighteen

KIDDY KARS

Our vantage point behind a low-slung fence gave us a spectacular view of the racetrack, highway signs, and numerous twists and turns beyond view. The year was 1979, and we were on the northern edge of Monterey Bay in Santa Cruz, California. I watched as the racers gripped their steering wheels in nervous anticipation. We all awaited the imminent starting bell, a sound that would unleash a fury of adrenaline and raw power in the race for the first turn.

The bell sounded. However, there was no cacophony of burning fuel and vaporizing rubber; there was only the slow-motion effect of a small group of tiny go-karts sputtering up a bumpy track and then vanishing behind the first winding curve. Two of the go-karts, one red and one blue, were being expertly handled, respectively, by our sons—Nathan, seven, and Isaiah, five.

The racers soon emerged from behind a small bluff. The red car (Nathan's) was leading Isaiah's blue car, which inspired our oldest to call out to his younger counterpart, "Catch me if you can!" Little Isaiah, however, seemed oblivious to the taunting. Instead, he appeared to be swept up and entirely captivated by the reality of operating a motor vehicle all by himself. The two tiny cars puttered onward at speeds that must have seemed supersonic to the boys.

As the race progressed, something caught my attention: the facial expressions of each boy. My older son showed signs of stress while my younger one seemed most delighted. Not only was Isaiah smiling broadly, but he had released his hands from the steering wheel and raised them in jubilation as if he were flying!

In contrast, Nathan was struggling with his steering wheel. Despite his intense efforts, the term "steering wheel" was a real misnomer because it had no effect whatsoever on the heading of the car, as all were linked to a central rail for safety's sake. He was very frustrated with this reality and powerless to control the direction of his journey. In turn, this epic struggle with the disconnected steering wheel was sapping his energy and his joy. I watched as he fought every twist and turn along the small track; he was missing all the fun of the ride.

My eldest was fighting a predetermined course; the youngest was embracing it. Although both boys were in the same position—traveling at the same speed in the same direction and passing the same scenery—their experience was profoundly different! In the end, neither the car nor its color, speed, direction, or track had much to do with the outcome, and nor did these external factors determine my sons' internal experience.

All these years later, I still struggle with my own disconnected steering wheel. When my life seems to take on a direction of its own and I proceed to struggle and resist, I try to recall that day at the amusement park. I think back to the powerful lesson I learned from two small boys driving around the Kiddy Kars track. One decided to valiantly fight and wrestle with that disconnected steering wheel, his predetermined fate. The other, releasing his grip and accepting his fate, enjoyed the entire ride.

In the end, it's always a matter of choice.

SMOOTH EVOLUTION

"Is my pearl as nice as yours, young man?"

It was a Saturday morning in 1998 in Palo Alto, California. The woman who had spoken appeared in front of the main jewelry counter at Neiman Marcus, looking toward me. At first glance, she was a frail silhouette, yet imbued with a grand energy; she had celebrated a life brimming with the full measure fortune had to offer.

Unfortunately, the second glance revealed a different tale, one of scuffled footwear, fraying garments, and a dilapidated diamond broach pinned to the bare lapel of her tattered topcoat. She embodied wealth's fleeting and fickle ways. Regardless, her smile arrested my soul, and her velvety voice soothed me like that of my favorite grandmother.

As she presented her hand to me much like jewelry models on the Home Shopping Network, I glanced down at the lifeless pearl bound in a tarnished mounting and rooted on a ring finger wrapped in thinning skin spotted with pigmentation. The ring, much like her hand, had traveled many miles. The pearl in my showcase to which she was referring was part of an extraordinarily rare and expensive collection of South Sea Pearls the store had brought in for a special three-day event. Each of the pearls in the collection started around twenty thousand dollars and went up from there. I glanced at the showcase, then at her hand, and finally up to her dusty blue eyes.

"Is it?" she repeated. "Is my pearl as nice as those?"

"Well," I began, tempted to go with the white lie. "Actually, no, yours isn't as nice as those, but I am quite sure that the oysters knew each other."

She raised her head and gave me a glorious smile. Then she said, "Thank you for that." She turned and left, and we never saw each other again. At least not in the flesh, for her angelic smile remained fixed in my thoughts for the remainder of that afternoon and weeks and months beyond. In the normal course of business, I would speak briefly to passing strangers such as her, but they came and went without much to distinguish their hundreds of faces and the quick exchanges. Forgetting the face and moving on to the next potential customer had, in fact, become habit.

This constant mental motion was disconnecting me from the customer (the human being) at hand; a sense of detachment allowed me to lock onto the next potential customer and press onward. By never deeply connecting with any one client, I clung to the belief that I would never be stuck with one, either. This became my agreement. It was like I had promised not to get too happy with success so I wouldn't be required to feel dismal with failure. In short, retail selling had become a perpetual quest for the next sale, the next potential client, the next opportunity, and the bigger, better prize just around the corner. After all, I had convinced myself, why get tangled up in all of this touchy-feely stuff? I just did my job, and my job was to sell.

Then, the casual contact with that lovely woman triggered a disturbance which rippled through my universe. The trusted retail armor had been breached by her reaction to my comments. All my protection was gone, and this woman had crashed through my protective walls and left me completely exposed. How had she done this to me?

The answer came hours later: whenever you speak to anybody, he or she turns into somebody. Even the slightest, briefest, most insignificant encounter with another human being, for whatever reason, has an effect on both parties. I thought about the effect I likely generated within the people whom I more or less brushed off in the interest of finding a better customer. Was I willing to take responsibility for every effect, no matter how small, that I might cause in others through my presence and energy? This single question transformed my role as a salesperson in a major way.

For years it had been my understanding that as a salesperson I was responsible for learning all of the features and benefits of my product and then relaying that information to prospects in a beautifully tailored sales presentation. I did not believe I was responsible for the customer's side of the sale, the so-called receiving side. My evolved view, however, is that I am responsible for 100 percent of sending and receiving information, which leaves the prospective client with absolutely zero responsibility in the sales presentation, which is as it should be.

It took me a long time to realize that throughout my entire sales career, I had only been focusing on half of the sale and leaving the other side in my customer's hands. It was a dangerous path—I was assuming that my clients were doing their part during my sales presentation, that they were diligently listening and assessing the product's features and benefits and weighing the facts. It was as if I was broadcasting a radio frequency but never bothered to make sure my clients had tuned their radios to my station. This acute awareness of my communication responsibility began to trigger a larger avenue of thought: could this awareness of customer communication create a transformation in my personal life—in real relationships—as well?

Indeed, sales and customer service lessons are imminently transferable. In fact, working with the public is precisely the place to develop these skills. Consider the endless migration of customers passing through our daily lives. Each interaction is an opportunity for us to improve our people skills, our communication skills, and our life skills.

Many eons ago in high school, I was snapped awake from a daydream with a dominant thought: two students can sit in this classroom for equal amounts of time while one gets a *failing grade* and one a *passing grade*.

It is the same in sales—by not really applying myself in class (with each customer) I was receiving no time benefit at all. All these decades later, as a manager of retail stores for some thirty years, I have come to realize that many employees seem to act the same way while they are at work.

The "at work" life is just a holding pattern until "real life" begins. How often do we hear (or say), "I can't wait for the weekend" or "Just three weeks until vacation!" While rejuvenation time is critical, we lose the *now* of life by wishing we were somewhere else. Isn't every hour at work just as precious and valuable as any other hour of our lives? Wasn't my interaction with that charming elderly lady about her pearls just as valuable as the time I spend with a buying customer? I believe the answer to both questions is a resounding *yes*. Wherever I am is a learning opportunity to be enjoyed.

I believe that is why we are put here on this earth. It is as if the people passing through our lives are a vast river that tumbles and bounces us off one another, and each encounter becomes a natural polishing process. Just like the pebbles in a riverbed, we are forever tossed and smoothed against one another by a constant power, its endless motion shaping our form.

As salespeople, we can view this process as our never-ending river of opportunity if we allow it to be. Each day, as we dip into the water we are offered another opportunity for personal growth and self-improvement. We encounter countless people along the way who present us with challenges, needs, and demands, all of which we must respond to. This forces us to hone our communication skills. One person might view this as work; I choose to embrace it as a process, a process of personal refinement.

The public agrees to enter though our door with their needs and challenges; we agree to use the opportunity to improve our ability to put others first. We improve our listening skills, stretch the boundaries of our patience, practice turning off our mental chatter, and really listen. In this way, all of the answers to personal improvement are right in front of us: it's our customers! We can choose to get a much greater value for the time we spend with them. This value far exceeds our pay, our bonus, our medical benefits, and our commissions. It is the value of appreciating the inherent worth of each person regardless of whether they choose to buy our product or not. We begin to view our customers beyond their role in providing us financial sustenance; they are the endless flow of force that smoothes our rough edges. They shape us. They help us evolve.

SMOOTH EVOLUTION

If the river can create beauty and smoothed stones through constant agitation and repetition, we can as well. Challenge shapes us and imparts lessons we can't learn any other way. That is, to improve ourselves we must engage with others. We can do this by viewing each human contact as an opportunity to enjoy others and also refine ourselves.

But what if our connection with a person is a negative experience? How can we glean value from that person? The answer is simple: we need to understand how to learn in both directions. One of my first jobs as a teenager was a brief stint at a surf shop near the beach in Capitola, California, renting surfboards to tourists. My job was to greet the customers and decide what type of equipment would be suitable. This quick assessment included a rough estimation of height, weight, and skill level. This part of the job was pretty easy. My boss, however, was a different story.

The owner was a gruff, chain-smoking man with a perpetual drip of perspiration trickling off his forehead and onto his puka shell necklace. The XXXL Hawaiian shirts he always wore could have doubled as circus tents. His hands were like two oven mitts, his eyebrows a tangle of coarse salt-and-pepper straw, and even his earlobes appeared weighted down as if fashioned from dense clay. No matter how I attempted to please him, he would explode in a rage over the tiniest annoyance. This was long before I acquired the skills I'm writing about here, so, of course, the boss and I never bonded. My tenure ended abruptly one morning as he and I stood gazing through the blue haze of cigarette smoke at a wall of surfing posters. Then he blurted, "I don't know why we aren't selling more of these posters." At that moment, I made a cardinal mistake—I offered my opinion.

"Well," I said, "in other surf shops they mount their posters in picture frames, and it really makes them look better. Maybe we could try that?"

I might as well have suggested that he should quit smoking, go on a diet, and take an anger management course, because he lurched towards me and said, "I've had it with you and your big opinions. You're fired!"

With the perspective of time, I realized years later that the most difficult people are also the greatest teachers, and my first boss taught me one of the most important lessons in management I've ever learned. Quite simply, I learned how *not* to treat people, and even more importantly, I learned the power of learning in both directions. Because I was on the receiving end of this man's wrath, I knew firsthand how it felt to be treated poorly. I vowed to myself that if I ever became a manager or owner of a business, I would always remember those feelings and the important lesson this man taught me that day.

In the end, we are each valuable and unique in some way. In dealing with other people, it's just a matter of how we perceive them, be they dressed in a faded Hawaiian shirt size XXXL or scuffed footwear, fraying garments, and a dilapidated diamond broach pinned on the bare lapel of a tattered topcoat. Each person teaches us something of value as they pass through our lives—lessons to improve the quality of our lives and the lives of those around us. Start noticing all the life lessons these people reveal. Once you do, your life will become one colossal classroom with thousands of teachers dedicated to the education of only one student: you.

Chapter Twenty

THE MISSING LINK

Like two synchronized swimmers, we swung open our respective taxi doors, stepped forward, and hit the back seat at the same moment.

"625 Madison, please," I said, "by the valet entrance at the hotel." ("Hotel" or some identifier other than "right side." The more information you give a New York cabbie, the better.)

"Why do you always get the easy customers?" my associate asked.

"You're referring to the sales presentation we just left, I suppose?"

"I am," he continued. "Your customers just seem to open up faster." He paused, looked out at the gathering clouds, and then added, "You just seem to hit it off with people."

I finished giving the driver directions, and we were off. "I'm flattered, but that really isn't the case."

"Maybe," my friend said, "but you are always chatting it up with everyone in the room from the moment you hit the door."

"I guess." While I thought about my friend's comment, I engaged in the ghastly task of excavating the grimy seat belt from between the deep folds of the seat. I cringed as my hand disappeared into a cold, evil blackness from which it might never return. Then I had it and pulled out the belt, riveted with fossilized bagel crumbs circa 1979.

"Anyway," I said, "let's look at the first few moments of that presentation. That client and I had never met before, and we didn't even discuss the product in the beginning."

"True, but you guys did go on and on about Hawaii."

"Right. If you recall, the client mentioned he had just returned from a vacation in Hawaii, so I encouraged him to share has story with us. That's all."

"Yeah, but that's my point," he mumbled. "Your customer has stories about climbing volcanoes and watching hot lava spew out. I get the clients who haven't seen a movie in the theater since *Rocky II*."

Ten minutes later, the taxi pulled to a stop. I decided to grab lunch before returning to my desk, and my associate sauntered off to bemoan his lack of interesting clients. Soon I found myself queued up and packed elbow to elbow at the local delicatessen. As the line inched toward the counter, I attempted to make a call on my cell phone.

Since I always power it off during sales presentations, I had to wait the few seconds while the gadget awakened and searched for a satellite signal. An obvious and logical thought popped into my head: attempting to conduct a conversation on a cell phone prior to it linking to a satellite is impossible. Before connecting, it's really nothing more than an electronic paperweight, and an ugly one, at that.

Then I had another painfully obvious but accurate thought: to begin speaking before the phone has made the proper connection would not only be foolish, it would be a complete waste of breath.

And then I realized where my mind-numbingly boring monologue was going—I'd just discovered "the missing link." It was right there in everyone's cell phone. I ordered, grabbed my sandwich, and continued my private little soliloquy as I walked along Madison Avenue. It was the answer to the question posed earlier during the taxi ride. At the beginning of every sales presentation, much like my cell phone, I begin by searching for a link to my client.

To begin a conversation with a customer, we should mimic the trusty cell phone. Search for and establish a link. Invest in those first critical moments with your client for establishing a connection and a path to easy communication. Search for subjects you may have in common—sports interests, professions, travel interests, or hobbies—things that link you and your client together in the briefest amount of time. Always be mindful that the subject matter should focus on them and their interests, not our own.

Customers will feel more comfortable about you and your product if at first they feel a genuine connection with you. And there's only one person responsible for establishing that connection: you. You are the cell phone with the search function.

Remember: those first few precious moments with your customer are not about your product, your service, yourself, or even selling. They are for *you* to go into search mode and make the connection with your clients. Remember to always find the missing link.

"Fortune assists the bold."
Virgil (70-19 B.C.E.)
Roman Poet

FEAR

The rising sun broke the horizon one morning as the young boy awoke to find two colossal figures sitting at the foot of his bed. Both clad in armor shining like onyx and steel in the cool light, the two towering sentries sat in silence.

Spying the weapons draped across their chest plates and the thick swords dangling at their sides, the boy's confidence surged—he would forever be protected by these two. He felt safe. Delighted, the young child could barely believe how closely they matched the template for which he'd hoped and prayed. Fearsome and menacing, the boy had invited the guardians into his life hours before during a bedtime prayer without weighing the devastating toll each would levy on his soul. It was a prayer for universal protection—an innocent child's prayer, a prayer to never face life alone.

They were to become his lifelong companions and faithful protectors, fighting fierce battles to protect the boy whenever he called upon their service. His two menacing protectors had eternal names: Fear and Worry.

For the next fifty years, the boy would live his life safely hidden behind his two protectors, rarely peeking from behind their armor to catch a glimpse of life's fearsome moments. That is, until the day the boy reached the age of fifty-five. On that day, he gathered up all of his courage and requested his guests leave him, for he was finally willing to go it alone. Just as easily as he'd conjured them decades before, his guardians vanished at his command.

Neither Fear nor Worry put up a fight. There was no argument, no resistance, not even an objection; each simply dissolved. They'd arrived by personal invitation and left the same way.

As for the fifty-five-year-old boy, he began to face life head-on for the very first time. He quickly came to realize that neither had provided much protection for him anyway. He had been hiding for his entire life behind vague apparitions pretending to be something greater. A new realization surged forth: he had actually been facing life's difficulties by himself all along, and he had done okay. This new truth began to permeate his being and fortify his soul.

For so long he could not have imagined living his life without the aid of his two hulking protectors. But just as easily as he had made them appear, he found new strength in dismissing them from his life. There was no cataclysmic event that triggered the shift, just an internal realization to step out of those old shadows. He held the power now, not they, just as he always had.

"A man is the sum of his actions, of what he has done, of what he can do. Nothing else."
Mahatma Gandhi

Chapter Twenty Two

PLANT IT FORWARD: A PATH TOWARD PASSION

You are your final destination. Sounds a bit strange, perhaps, but that is the powerful theme and belief that embodied the life of one John Chapman, born September 26, 1774, in Massachusetts. You may not recognize the birth name, but you are no doubt familiar with this American.

His is the tale of an educated, young bachelor with visions of apple orchards in full bloom greeting settlers as they pushed west; his is the legend of the man we all know as Johnny Appleseed, who found his passion and set out to personally plant a welcome mat of apple blossoms across Illinois, Indiana, Kentucky, Pennsylvania, and Ohio. Scattering seeds that later become apple blossoms, this single human being provided beauty, joy, and promise to young families as they forged into an uncertain new world.

As a young child, I was captivated by the story of Johnny Appleseed.

To this day, some 220 years after Johnny Appleseed traveled barefoot across the plains, descendants of his original trees still grace this land. Indeed, hundreds of years after his death, his spirit still reverberates down through generations. In a world where billions of lives are lived, spent, and quickly forgotten, how is it that certain people are long remembered and immortalized, even after they are physically gone?

Certain extraordinary people have an ability to rise above the din of humanity and touch the hearts and souls of future generations. In some cases, these same people amass great fortunes of wealth and possessions, and in many cases, they do not. But almost without exception, all discover a simple, singular path to their calling and life's work: passion. Likewise, this path to passion can be a simple, direct route for everyone.

One human myth is that such a discovery requires exhaustive effort and traveling great distances to sit with bearded sages atop pristine mountain peaks. This true self, goes the myth, must be hidden somewhere "out there," always just beyond reach, always as elusive as the next bend in the road or the next wise master dispensing precious pearls. But what if there was nowhere to go and nothing to do in order to find your passion and your calling in life? What if your true calling was not "out there," but it was already planted within you as undiscovered seeds of passion? Well, if that were true, then instead of searching you would only have to begin acting as though you were already a complete and gifted human being (which you are!).

Could this be the long-lost secret of the ages? Simply acting as if you were already a complete, valued, and gifted human being would make you the starting point and the finishing line to your own journey. Yes, indeed—you are your final destination.

Consider this: Suppose the universal spirit granted you a gift at birth and then placed you in a specific moment in time on earth to live your life. Would a benevolent, all-knowing presence place you a great distance from your gift and gain enjoyment from watching you struggle for years to find it? Or would this loving parent simply hand you the gift so that they could enjoy and share it immediately? The notion that we each need to search for our entire lives to find our gifts is erroneous. A powerful new belief would be to consider, once and for all, that your gift was factory installed on day one, and that any answer you need is, of course, you, courtesy of the universe. It's really that simple.

Let's go back to our vagrant Johnny Appleseed. What was his passion and gift? More importantly, how did he share that gift with others? At first glance, the obvious answer might be that he loved trees. Being an arborist was his singular passion. But a larger passion of his was people: the settlers and families moving west. The apple trees are tangible evidence of Johnny Appleseed's internal passion—the comfort, joy, and hope he wished to bestow on so many. The apple trees, it turns out, were simply a means of sharing his passion.

So what about you? What means or methods are you employing to share your gift and your passion with those you meet? Think about this: what "trees" are you planting, consciously or unconsciously, that might bloom for the joy and comfort of others today, tomorrow, and decades from now? There is a lot of press these days about our carbon footprint and the effect humans have on the planet. Additionally, I'd like each of us to embrace and be responsible for the "heart print" we leave on earth after we are physically gone. Some people in our past, knowingly or unknowingly, planted their trees in our garden. These trees provide a cooling shade against the harsh sunlight of life, or perhaps they're overgrown and blocking the view of all that is beautiful. Maybe their roots have become overreaching and troublesome to us.

The question becomes, "What steps should you take now to start the process of changing the quality of your life and the lives of countless souls in future generations?"

- Step One: Search Your Garden. Carefully remove any trees planted in your past, no matter who planted them, that block your view to the person you are capable of becoming and the person you deserve to be. Don't let someone else's influence blot out your best you. Clear your horizon of any tree that stops you from seeing yourself as a gifted, valued, loving human being.

- Step Two: Plant New Trees. That's right; it's your garden, so just plant bold, towering trees of hope, joy, and light. Create your very own Garden of Eden.

- Step Three: Monitor Your Trees. Consider the trees you have planted, are planting, and will plant in the lives of your loved ones, friends, passersby, and anyone and everyone with whom you come into contact. Each contact with another human being, no matter how brief, is like planting a seed in his or her life. It blossoms into a chain of events, even if only in a small way.

Where does this chain of events end? Does it end? I don't believe we actually comprehend how far our sphere of influence extends. I do know that there were things that were done or said to me as a small child that still influence me to this day. And if those "trees" were troublesome to me, I've worked hard to remove them. Now, as I go about the joyful business of raising my own children and spending time with my grandchildren, I am highly aware of the seeds I plant within them.

- Step Four: Nurture Your Trees. Take responsibility for the trees you plant. Carefully nurture, water, and fertilize the ones you want to grow. Trim them and keep them neat. Allow your inner peace to stem from your eternal effect. We are each a living branch on an endless growth of humanity's past souls and souls yet to come, stretching through eternity as we momentarily cling to the power of life and influence. Seize this power; it belongs to you now!

Your inner power, your gift and passion, was granted to you as something unique and precious. Decide what you will do with it and what choices you will make. Choose to plant seeds that will blossom into future generations. Take full responsibility for the seeds you plant and the effect they have on others. Choose to plant positive seeds in every encounter with other human beings. Let the fruit of your efforts influence the future in a positive way. Life is colossal, and you are a big part of it. This is your time.

In the first chapter of this book, I made you a promise: your passion will produce boundless motivation. We shared the idea that the source of passion is love. In coming full circle, this love, too, comes to us as a gift, passed down from generation to generation to be learned, nurtured, shared, and then passed along to the future by its current caretaker: you.

That's right—we do not even own the *love* we feel. We simply carry it along with us in this fragile vessel we know as our body. We have the power to take these seeds within, plant love everywhere, and quench the thirst of others along our way. Your path to passion starts with love—first for yourself, and then for others.

Go now in love. Find passion and plant those seeds everywhere you go. We will all be richer from your time here, as will future generations. You will move through this life with a quiet peace few ever know.

These are the treasured gifts of a life well lived.

Q&A

Why Contagious Passion*?*

If one wants to make a statement to the universe, the statement must be universal, which is the theme of *Contagious Passion*. Rather than burdening my readers with another set of selling rules and conditions to enhance their ability to communicate, I elected to reveal a method of communication everyone in the world already possesses.

Sort of like the saying, "A straight line is the shortest distance between two points?"

Exactly; I knew if I created the awakening in my reader, then he need only grasp the concepts and begin tapping into his own power source instantly, even before reading the entire book.

Why did Contagious Passion *contain a story about finding your true color?*

Because we must operate in life from our core persona, our true self; this is the only way to genuinely connect with others.

Why "Father?" How does this story fit into a sales book?

"Father" is a story to remind us all how we must appreciate every precious moment we have and be fully alive and engaged in that moment. "Father" is the true story of the passing of Alfred W. Wheeler, my wife's father. This man embraced me as his own son and taught me the true meaning of what it is to hold the title of "father." And to always remember that *tempus fugit,* i.e., time flies.

Tell me more about Otis ("Put a Shine on the Day").

Otis was one of those extraordinary people who are all around us but we often miss. Although we only knew each other for three years, he and I spoke daily. The amount of wisdom this man possessed, coupled with his willingness to share it (not to mention his warm personality), was an inspiration to me on so many levels. Otis passed away a number of years ago, but I can still conjure his radiant smile and hear his rich voice whenever I need him.

Was "Invisible People" a turning point in your life?

Definitely. I think if there was only one message to be gained from reading *Contagious Passion*, it should be this: notice every person in your life!

Overall, what do you hope your readers will take away from Contagious Passion? *And what inspired you to write it?*

Love. I use to go around telling everyone that I wrote my book to "trick people into happiness!" Of course I wanted them to read it and vastly improve their selling abilities. More importantly, however, I wanted them to realize the connection between improving one's sales abilities and one's life relationships. That paradigm shift is life changing.

So you want to change lives?

Not exactly; what I want is to provide the insights, tools, and revelations required for individuals to take this important life-changing step for themselves.

EPILOGUE

There must be a million people here.

Oh, there's a lot more than that.

Really? How many do you think there are?

"Think?" Young man, please.

Sorry, I forgot; how many are there?

Thank you. There are 5,078,414.

Wow … amazing. That many? Oops. Sorry.

Remember, this was over a seventy-four-year period.

Yeah, but it still seems impossible. So many people; it's hard for me to believe. I mean, I believe. Don't think I don't.

I know you do. You always did, and that's why you're seeing all of this today.

Thanks again for that.

You're very welcome.

It's kind of sad now that I look at them all, you know, all of them standing in front of me like this, each of them a complete person. And each one of them had a full life, good times, bad times, pleasures, and pains just like I did.

That's right.

Why is it I didn't start noticing them until I turned fifty-one?

Well, you did a lot better than some people, who never notice anything except what's for dinner and who's going to make the playoffs.

And you're telling me that you actually sent every one of these people into my life at just the right moment to have an effect on me and for me to have an effect on them?

That was the plan.

How did I do? I mean … I guess I mean, how did I do with all of them from your perspective?

Well, just like most people, you started life looking out for number one. Not to worry; I expect it. But as time goes on, I'm hopeful maturity sets in and begins to expand your world. Empathy. Humility. I'm hopeful you begin to notice each individual person in a different light. Now, most people never get to the final level, but when you realize that everyone in the world is connected, you've come full circle.

Everyone matters.

Everyone matters.

Each connection with each person I've come into contact with over a lifetime—it was all planned?

That's why I put them there.

Five million … how many again?

5,078,414. It's different for everyone. Let me tell you—air travel has really bumped up people's life totals.

But I met them one at a time. That's how I missed most of them; it was just one at a time. So what you're telling me is that there was never a person who came through my life, no matter however briefly, no matter how insignificantly …

Yes, not a single one who wasn't sent to you by me. That's exactly what I'm telling you; I sent every single one.

This changes everything, doesn't it?

I would hope so.

All of it a majestic plan from your universal mind.

Yes, and had you known, how might you have acted and reacted to each person you meet in a lifetime?

And that was a part of the plan, too, right? Because what we do and say when we don't know someone is watching is really the measure of our character.

I think you've got the hang of this now.

I can't believe I'm going to say this, but it all makes sense.

And it always did; you just didn't have the luxury of seeing the full picture.

Wow.

I hear that a lot. That's right up there with "unbelievable."

Is it time, then?

It is time, my dear child.

Thank you.

No, thank you.

For what?

For seeing.

ACKNOWLEDGMENTS

I have a confession to make. I rarely read the acknowledgment page in any book. After all, it's just a long list of the names of people I will never meet, right? Wrong.

It wasn't until I began this endeavor that I realized just how valuable that list of names really is for the author and, ultimately, for the reader. I now fully understand how most books would never get to print without this list of names, and my book is no different. Behind each moniker is a caring soul who picked me up when I stumbled, dusted me off, and encouraged me to press onwards to the finish line. That said, I am also a changed man and will now read the acknowledgment page in every book I open; if you've made it this far I'm hopeful you'll do the same here. I would like to thank all of the following people.

Joseph "JoJo" Wheeler, who introduced me to the wonderful world of words. Federico Richards, who supported and encouraged me during the first trembling stages of this endeavor. Author Landon J. Napoleon, for his masterful editing, personal involvement, and warm friendship along my journey.

Ann Herrias, for editing, and Harry Lee, for his tireless proofreading. Johi Paulson, for her amazing cover design, formatting, and illustrations. John Chambers, who inspired me through a causal conversation to trust in myself and share my thoughts and feelings with the world. Matthew Morris, editor-in-chief for *Revolution* magazine, for his wonderful words of encouragement.

A very special thanks to Carol Olson, for her ongoing faith in me from the very beginning. She was a champion for my cause who believed in my abilities and invested her time, talent, and passion into this project; I am forever indebted. All my friends and colleagues at The Swatch Group, Neiman Marcus, and Bulgari U.S.A. I learned from you all.

To my lovely wife Mary and our three children, Isaiah, Emily, and Nathan, for their constant support, love, and encouragement. To my granddaughters Portia, Chloe, Avery, and Reese for reminding me to always view life through the eyes of a child.

And, finally, to all who have attended one of my seminars and especially those of you who took the time to stay afterwards to share kind words of support and encouragement—you all had a hand in bringing this book to its completion, and I thank you for that. I cherish each one of you more than words can express.

AUTHOR BIO

Jeff Cox was born in 1952 in Santa Cruz, California. He has been actively involved in sales and sales training for more than thirty-five years. He still lives in the San Francisco Bay Area with his wife, two sons, daughter, and four granddaughters. *Contagious Passion* is his first book.

Manufactured By: RR Donnelley
                     Momence, IL USA
                     February, 2011